Beyond the
Rainbow Warrior

A COLLECTION OF
STORIES TO CELEBRATE
25 YEARS OF
GREENPEACE

Beyond the Rainbow Warrior

Edited by
Michael Morpurgo

Art edited by
Michael Foreman

PAVILION

This edition published in Great Britain in 1996 by
PAVILION BOOKS LIMITED
26 Upper Ground, London SE1 9PD

A CIP catalogue record for this book
is available from the British Library.

ISBN 1 85793 888 7 (cased)
ISBN 1 86205 035 X (limp)

Text set in Stempel Garamond
Printed and bound in Spain by Bookprint

2 4 6 8 10 9 7 5 3 1

This book may be ordered by post direct from the publisher.
Please contact the Marketing Department.
But try your bookshop first.

Contents

Introduction

FOR TWENTY-FIVE YEARS now, Greenpeace has been trying to save the planet, trying to save us from ourselves. Few organisations can have done more to concentrate the public mind on the holocaust we seem intent on inflicting upon our world. It is they who have stood between big business interests and the massacre of our fellow creatures, who have sailed their fragile boats in amongst the armadas of nations to bring a stop to their despoiling of the earth. Their physical courage and their tenacity against all odds has touched our hearts, and much more importantly, has opened our eyes too.

They were not the first to cry a halt to the destruction of the natural world. Many extraordinary organisations and individuals have dedicated themselves to that end. But they are certainly the most heroic. They are the rainbow warriors of our time. Many writers too have taken up the cudgel. From *Moby Dick*, to *Tarka the Otter*, to *The Iron Man*, writers have crafted their tales of man's obsessive hunting, of his insatiable greed, of his increasing ruination of the world. Television documentaries have brought into our homes the intimate lives of almost every creature and plant known to man. Never was the human race more aware of its surroundings. And yet, and yet . . .

We seem more and more to have detached ourselves from our fellow creatures, feeling less and less part of the natural world where we live and from which we grew. Our awareness is as mere observers, delighting in landscape as if it were a picture, in pandas and orang-utans as if they were mere cuddly exhibits.

Here in this book, are nine writers who write not as observers, but as beings amongst beings in sympathy with, in empathy with their world. You will find no 'tales of sound and fury', no polemics, but rather nine totally different ways of telling the same story, a story that 'signifies' everything.

Michael Morpurgo

Dragon Soup

ANTHONY HOROWITZ

Illustrated by Quentin Blake

THE KNIGHT and his boy had been riding now for three days although they had only one horse between them. For most of the time the boy had been seated behind his master. Sometimes he followed him on foot. And sometimes they walked together to allow the horse some rest. They had spoken little: the knight because he was thinking of the immensity of the task that lay ahead, the boy because he was not meant to speak unless the knight spoke to him first.

The knight was a tall, thin man – rather too tall and thin, in fact, for the armour he was wearing. From a distance he must have looked a bit like a silver lobster. He was about thirty years old which, at the time of this story, was really quite old indeed as people didn't tend to live long lives. There were always wars to die in or diseases to die of and even a simple quarrel could quickly turn into a duel to the death. The knight had a lop-sided but handsome face spoiled only by his unusually pale skin. It had been pale ever since the king had told him what he had to do. His name was Sir Jolyon.

The boy was, of course, the knight's page and his name was Gawain. He was thirteen years old but would not have been able to count that far as he had had no education at all. He couldn't read and could only write five letters of his name (he still had trouble with the w). He was, however, an expert at polishing armour and looking after the horse and he was also a good cook. Gawain had straw-coloured hair, bright blue eyes and surprisingly good teeth. People said he looked like his father, but as he had never met his father he couldn't be sure.

In the three days that they had been travelling, their path had taken them away from the king's castle and across the valley to the great river that bordered the king's land. They had crossed the river, both of them clinging to the horse which was the only one of them that could swim, and after passing through a small and squalid village – all dung heaps and delapidated huts – they had plunged into The Eternal Forest. At least that was what it was called. For two days they had barely seen the sunlight at all. The trees were so close together that they seemed to be tied into knots and their feet made no sound on the bed of earth and mouldy leaves.

On the evening of the third day they stopped and Gawain made a bonfire while his master rested against a tree. Once the fire was lit, Gawain went out and managed to catch two hedgehogs which he cooked into a delicious meal with roots and vegetables he had brought from the castle. Sir Jolyon opened a flagon of wine and the two of them sat together, close to the flames, their shadows flickering on the trees behind them.

'You've never seen a dragon,' Sir Jolyon said suddenly, breaking the silence.

'No, sir,' Gawain replied. 'But Meg used to tell me about them.'

'That old witch!' Meg was a so-called wise woman, living just inside the castle walls. People went to her when they were ill or when they were desperate and she had a potion for everything. Not that the potions ever really worked.

'They are terrible animals,' Sir Jolyon went on. 'Not so much animals as monsters. They have wings but they're not birds. They have scales but they're not fish. They have terrible teeth and razor-sharp claws and a long, swishy tail they can use to beat you to death if they haven't torn you apart first.' He shivered and held his hand out to the flames.

'Why do you have to kill this dragon?' Gawain asked.

'Because the king told me to!' The knight sighed. He was not a particularly brave man and had hoped to see his old age . . . thirty-five or six. 'It's a great honour to have been chosen,' he added. 'I will kill the dragon and my name will go down in all the songs and poems. Sir Jolyon the Dragon Slayer. And, of course, I'll be invited to a feast and I'll sit next to the queen and you know what will be served.'

'Dragon soup,' Gawain said.

'Yes. Dragon soup.' Sir Jolyon fell silent, thinking about the rich green broth and wondering if it would taste nicer than the hedgehog he was eating now. Not that hedgehog was bad. Just a bit . . . spiky. Once he had killed the dragon he would have to cut off its head and bring it back to the castle to be made into soup. This would be the proof that he had killed it (the proof, as it were, of the pudding) and anyway, dragon soup was a great speciality. Although Sir Jolyon himself had never tasted it, he knew that lords and ladies from all over the kingdom would congregate in the castle to share the steaming bowl and he would be the guest of honour. Provided, of course, that he had survived.

'I still don't understand why you have to kill it,' Gawain muttered.

'What do you mean?' Sir Jolyon snapped, feeling a little annoyed. 'It's a dragon! I just told you! It's been terrorizing the kingdom. Everybody knows it has to die.'

'Meg says that dragons are full of magic,' Gawain said. 'She also says that there aren't many of them left . . .'

'What does Meg know?' Sir Jolyon glared at his page and Gawain bit his tongue, wondering if the knight would beat him. Sir Jolyon was a kindly man and only beat him occasionally but the occasions were usually just like this. The last thing a page should do was argue with his master. After all, he was only allowed to talk at all as a special treat.

But maybe the thought of his meeting with the dragon had softened Sir

Jolyon. He threw a hedgehog leg into the flames and shook his head. 'Dragons are a nuisance and a danger and it's the duty of a knight to be rid of them,' he explained. 'Anyway,' he added, 'this dragon has taken a beautiful princess as its prisoner. She has been seen, chained to its cave. Once the dragon is dead, I'll be able to free her.'

'Will the princess marry you?' Gawain asked.

'I expect so.' Sir Jolyon nodded. 'I must say, it would be nice to be married. I'd like to have children of my own. And women are better cooks than boys.'

Gawain wasn't sure this was true but decided he'd argued enough. He fell silent and soon the two of them slept.

The next day they travelled on again and soon they reached the other side of The Eternal Forest. Gawain did mutter that obviously it wasn't eternal after all and this time Sir Jolyon clipped him on the ear and told him that the name was poetic not geographic and Gawain said nothing more.

But the far side of the wood was a depressing place. It was as if there had been a dreadful storm there. As far as the eye could see, trees had been torn down, the bare and broken stumps left slanting out of the ground like a monstrous shipwreck. Even in the depths of the forest they had been heartened by birdsong and by the bright splashes of colour of butterflies and flowers. But here everything was grey and silent and even the horse seemed sad as it clip-clopped its way through the great emptiness.

'You see, Gawain!' Sir Jolyon said, 'we must be getting close to the dragon. Look at all the destruction it's wrought! Now do you think it's so magical?'

A few minutes later they came upon a peasant, scrabbling amongst the tree-stumps, collecting wood for a fire. You could tell he was a peasant because he was dressed in rags and covered from head to foot in dung. He was also very short. Because of their notoriously poor diet, peasants seldom grew tall.

'Good morrow, my man!' Sir Jolyon called out.

'Good day, my lord!' The peasant dropped all his wood and cowered. 'You're not going to kill me, are you, my lord?'

'No!' Sir Jolyon replied.

'That's all right then.' The peasant let out a deep sigh. 'It's just that you never know . . .'

'It is the dragon that I have come to kill,' Sir Jolyon explained.

'Dragon? What dragon is that, my lord?'

'The dragon that was responsible for all this.' Sir Jolyon waved a hand over the ruins of the forest.

'That wasn't any dragon!' The peasant shook his head. 'That was the people from the city.'

'The city?'

'It's on the other side of the hills.' The peasant pointed vaguely to the west. 'They keep coming out here in their carts. They need the wood, you see. Wood for their houses. Wood for their furniture. And wood for their carts, for that matter. They've got wooden shops where they sell wood. And some of them have got wooden teeth.' The peasant shook his head. 'The way things are going, there soon won't be any wood left, if you ask me. But of course nobody asks me because I'm just a peasant.'

'But what about the dragon?' Sir Jolyon demanded.

'I haven't seen any dragon,' the peasant replied.

Sir Jolyon glanced at Gawain but said nothing. For his part, Gawain did his best not to look too pleased with himself in an 'I told you so' sort of way. But he wasn't entirely successful.

The two of them rode on.

A few hours later they had left the ruined forest behind them but now they found themselves in a place that was even more desolate. Thick black

clouds hung in the air, stifling the sun, and there was a stench of burning. The ground was black, too. What little grass there was had lost all its colour and sprouted in small, ugly patches. Here and there black liquid oozed out of the soil like blood from a poisoned wound. Gawain had to hold a handkerchief over his mouth. He was finding it difficult to breathe.

'Now the dragon must be close!' Sir Jolyon gasped. 'You can see what its breath has done to the land. It's well-known that dragons breathe fire and that the fire destroys everything it touches. Now you can see for yourself . . .'

'This wasn't any dragon!' a voice remarked.

Sir Jolyon twisted round in his saddle and was rather annoyed to see that the peasant had followed them from the edge of the Eternal Forest. Or maybe it was a second peasant. It was hard to say as really every peasant looked more or less the same. 'Then what was it?' he demanded.

'It's those city folk,' the peasant explained. 'Things haven't been the same round here since they discovered oil. They dig it up and as if that doesn't do enough damage, they burn it in their houses and castles and the smoke goes everywhere. And then there are the oil spillages. You should see what happens when two cart-loads of oil collide! And of course, everyone blames everyone else and nothing ever gets done. It's not very pleasant being a peasant round here, I can tell you.'

Once again, Sir Jolyon said nothing. He and Gawain rode on.

And so it was that on the fifth day they finally reached the dragon's cave. This time there could be no mistake. The cave was set into a rocky hillside, partly hidden by a clump of wild olive trees. Outside the cave, the ground was strewn with bones, picked white by the birds. Whether they were human or animal, Gawain could not say. There was no sign of the dragon but the princess was there, just as Sir Jolyon had said. She was as beautiful as a princess ought to be, with long blond hair curling over her shoulders and slender arms and legs. She was dressed in a simple white dress that fell to her ankles with a gold band high up one arm. And she was chained to the rock. Sir Jolyon had been right about that, too. Both her wrists were attached to silver chains which glinted in the sun. She was standing very still, as if she were afraid to move.

'You see!' Sir Jolyon whispered. 'The dragon has taken a princess as his prisoner, just like I said.'

'It certainly looks that way,' Gawain admitted.

'What other explanation could there be?' Sir Jolyon snapped. He was still feeling uncertain of himself after the wood and the oil. 'The lady's in chains. The lady's a prisoner. And it's my job to rescue her. My sword.'

Gawain jumped off the horse and removed his master's sword from its oilskin wrapping. The sword was a very precious item. Sir Jolyon's father had been killed by it in one battle and his grandfather had been killed by it in another. You could say, in fact, that the sword had not only run *in* the family but *through* it as well. The sword was almost as long as Gawain was high and it also weighed a great deal. Gawain managed to balance it on his arm only with difficulty and was grateful when Sir Jolyon reached down and took it.

'And now,' said Sir Jolyon, 'God willing, we rescue the princess. Death to the dragon! Glory and dragon soup for me!'

'Amen,' Gawain muttered. That was what he was meant to say.

The two of them walked up the hill making as little noise as possible which wasn't easy as Sir Jolyon's armour clinked and clattered and the sword was so heavy he had to drag it some of the way. But, as it happened, it wasn't the princess who heard them first. It was the dragon.

Just as they reached the cave, there was a movement and the dragon appeared. Sir Jolyon fell back, clasping his sword. Even Gawain stopped dead in his tracks and gasped.

The dragon was smaller than he had expected but much more

dangerous and deadly-looking. 'Monster' was the first word that came into his head. But at the same time he knew it was something much, much more.

It was a dazzling green. He had never seen a green like it: dark and yet somehow luminescent. It had a long neck (and that made him think of a snake) and yet it had four wings which reminded him of a bat and a butterfly and at the same time of a silk kite he had once seen flying over the castle. The dragon had the most wonderful eyes. They were green too and shone like emeralds. It did have scales but these didn't remind Gawain so much of a snake. They reminded him more of Sir Jolyon himself. It was as if the dragon had come to meet them dressed in green armour.

But even as he marvelled at the creature's strange beauty, he couldn't avoid trembling at its savagery and strength. The dragon had been designed to kill and Gawain remembered the clean white bones that littered the hillside. Its legs and arms ended with vicious, curling claws. Its tail, forked at the end, writhed and twisted on the ground. Jagged teeth surrounded the dark cave of its mouth. Two plumes of smoke rose from its nostrils and as Gawain stared, a tongue of flames suddenly shot out, singeing the morning air.

Gawain couldn't have moved if he'd wanted to. And he did want to! Given a choice he would have turned and run away but that would have meant abandoning his master and that was one thing a page could never do. If there had been a rule book for pages, in fact, this would have been on the first page. For his part, Sir Jolyon seemed to have come together for the first time in his life. He actually looked brave. As the terrible creature advanced towards him, he lifted his sword in both hands and prepared to strike.

'Stop!'

Gawain and Sir Jolyon swung round. At first neither of them could believe it. But it was true. The cry had come from the princess.

Sir Jolyon faltered, the sword hovering above his shoulders.

'Put it down!' the princess insisted.

Sir Jolyon glanced at the dragon. It was getting closer and closer and already it was close enough. If it so much as sneezed, the knight would be ashes.

'Put your sword down and leave it alone!' the princess cried out.

'But . . . but . . . I've come to rescue you!' Sir Jolyon explained.

'I don't need rescuing. If anyone needs rescuing, it's the dragon.' The princess fumbled with the chains which instantly fell off her wrists. At once she ran over to the dragon, placing herself between it and Sir Jolyon's sword.

The knight stared at her. The page didn't trust himself to speak.

'You should be ashamed of yourself,' the princess said. 'Why do you want to kill the dragon?' What harm has it ever done to you?'

'Well . . .' Sir Jolyon stammered.

'Dragons are wonderful creatures,' the princess went on. 'There's nothing on the planet like them. And now they're an endangered species . . . mainly because of idiots like you who've gone round the place destroying them.' She put her arm round the dragon's neck. It murmured softly, a bit like a large pussy cat, Gawain thought.

'What about all the bones?' Sir Jolyon demanded. 'There are bones everywhere.'

'Lamb bones. And ham bones. The dragon has to eat and so do I. We leave them out so that the birds can get a share. It's called recycling!'

'But . . . you were being kept prisoner!' Sir Jolyon exclaimed. 'We saw you! Chained to the rock!'

'I chained myself as a protest!' the princess replied. She stopped and blushed. 'Yes, I suppose it could have been misinterpreted, now I think about it. But I was trying to make a point.'

'A point?'

'Yes. Just because you don't understand something, it doesn't mean you have to kill it. And just think of a world without dragons! I think it would be a much sadder, less magical place.'

Sir Jolyon had been holding his weapon up throughout all this but now his sword-arm gave way and he allowed it to fall to the ground. Gawain stepped forward. 'Shall I put it away?' he asked.

'Yes. Yes.' Sir Jolyon looked at the dragon with mixed feelings. He could see now that the princess was right. It was a remarkable creature and it certainly meant him no harm. It was still purring quietly while the princess stroked its neck. At the same time, though, he was depressed. He wasn't going to be a hero after all. Nobody would put him in their poems or sing about him in their songs. And there was something rather worse. He had failed the king. The king would not be pleased.

'You'd better come in,' the princess said.

'All right,' Sir Jolyon agreed.

With Gawain right behind him and the dragon bringing up the rear, Sir Jolyon went into the cave. It was actually a great deal warmer and more welcoming than he would have believed. There were carpets, comfortable chairs, occasional tables and even a small window with home-made curtains. The princess served mead from a large pot hung over the fire while the dragon curled up in a corner. Gawain chose the corner opposite and sat down and listened while the adults talked.

'It's no good,' Sir Jolyon exclaimed. 'The king must have his dragon soup. I can't go back empty-handed!'

'Dragon soup!' The princess wrinkled her nose. 'What does it taste like?'

'I've never tried it myself,' Sir Jolyon replied. 'But I understand it's a bit like chicken and a bit like fish. It's got a smokey flavour, too. But the main thing is, it's the most glorious green. I think people eat it as much for the colour as for the taste.

'But you're not going to kill the dragon, are you?' the princess asked.

'No. You've talked me out of that. But we're going to have to do something. If the king believes the dragon is still alive, he'll send someone else to do the job. And if he finds out I failed him on purpose, he'll probably have me killed at the same time.'

It was then that Gawain broke the second rule of pages. He spoke without being addressed first. 'Can I make a suggestion?' he asked.

The knight and the princess turned as one. 'Go on,' Sir Jolyon muttered. 'Although I doubt you can help.'

'Let me go back to the palace,' Gawain said. 'I know what dragon soup should taste like and I'm sure I can make something similar. I'll tell the king that you're dead. Obviously he'll think that the dragon is dead. And then in two weeks' time I'll slip away and come back – nobody will bother me – and with a bit of luck all four of us will be able to live here in peace.'

'You're a brave boy,' the princess exclaimed. 'I think you should certainly give it a try.'

'I suppose it can't hurt,' Sir Jolyon said. 'But I don't think there's any chance that it will work.

Gawain rode off the following morning. Sir Jolyon, the princess and the dragon watched him until he was just a speck in the distance. Then they went back into the cave.

In the days that followed, Sir Jolyon enjoyed what was certainly the happiest time of his life. Naturally enough, he fell in love with the princess. But perhaps more surprisingly he also fell in love with the dragon. The three of them went for long walks, ate picnics in the hills and swam in the clear water of the local lake. Sir Jolyon also discovered dragon-flying. This was incredibly exciting. Holding on to the dragon's shoulders he would be lifted high into the air. The dragon could fly at up to fifty miles per hour, faster than any living creature and Sir Jolyon would yell with delight as he was pulled up, right up to the clouds and then down again, hurtling towards the earth and only curving at the last minute, just missing the tops of the trees.

He and the princess, whose name was Penelope, talked late into the night and Sir Jolyon told her about the peasant he had met and about the broken wood and the oil. It was then that the two of them had an idea. They would form an organization, a sort of club for all the people who cared about the planet; about the plants that grew on it and the creatures that lived on it. This seemed like a very good idea indeed. The only trouble was, they couldn't think of a name for it. Sir Jolyon (being a knight) suggested The Global Nobles but Penelope thought that was too elitist and preferred The Round Table, an idea which was eventually used by somebody else.

They spent many more days talking about the name but as time passed they became too worried to think about it further. For almost three weeks had passed and there was still no sign of Gawain. Now Sir Jolyon became convinced that the page had somehow fallen foul of the king and blamed himself for letting the boy go back. Any day now he expected to see a whole squadron of knights galloping up the hill to claim their prize. He was even more worried about the dragon than he was about himself.

But then, on the nineteenth day, Gawain reappeared on the horse, bringing with him all of Sir Jolyon's and his own possessions. He had assumed, rightly as it turned out, that the two of them would continue to live with the princess in the cave.

He also brought a large bowl of dragon soup.

Gawain was, you will recall, a good cook and that night Sir Jolyon and Princess Penelope sat down to taste the rich broth that had completely fooled the king and his court. And it was delicious; bright green, and full of flavour.

'All right!' Sir Jolyon exclaimed when he had tasted a mouthful. 'Tell me, Gawain. How did you make it?'

Penelope nodded. The dragon eyed the boy suspiciously.

'It was easy,' Gawain explained. 'I used cod for the taste of fish and two capons for the flavour of chicken. I added onions, carrots, turnips and lentils to thicken it out. I gave it a good pinch of cayenne pepper for the dragon's fire and some burned bacon for the dragon's smoke. Finally I stirred in a good measure of brandy so nobody would ask too many questions. And there you have it. Dragon soup!'

'That's brilliant,' Penelope said. 'But there's one thing you've forgotten. The colour! How did you make it this glorious shade of green?'

'That was the easiest thing of all,' Gawain replied. 'I added several pounds of green peas.'

'Green peas,' Sir Jolyon muttered. For some reason it seemed to ring a bell. He turned to the princess. 'Now that gives me an idea,' he said.

Nelson's Chair

Joan Aiken

Illustrated by Alan Marks

AFTER THE death of Nelson Far-eye, the State Department closed down the Government Department at Fort Pilgrim, Maryland, which had gone under the name of Psychovisuals Unit A. Nelson Far-eye had been ninety-three years of age, none of the others in the section had anything like his gift, and his death coincided with a period of stringent economies and cut-backs; education services were being sharply reduced, coffee-making equipment was sold off, and gardeners told that, if they wanted to keep their jobs, they must learn to work on a computerized basis.

The loss of Nelson was irreparable; but not so bad as it would have been thirty years earlier.

Nelson Inogaat Far-eye, part Navajo, part Inuit, had been a psycho-telergist of immense and unmatched powers; he could pass his finger across a map and detect in it Aztec ruins or a crumbling radioactive submerged nuclear submarine; he would listen to a faint radio cheep and locate its origin, however far distant, in this world or some other; he could scrutinize a picture and slowly absorb from it not only the name, nationality and sex of the painter, and where, and when, it had been done, but also, if it were a portrait, the identity and age of the sitter, even though the painting might be hundreds or thousands of years old.

Now all this ability and insight was switched off and whisked away, who knew where? and the State Department, less concerned these days about the location of nuclear submarines, and wishful to cut down on administrative expenses, had decided to close the Psychovisuals Unit, on the grounds that, as it didn't cost very much anyway (seven old gentlemen sitting in silence round a map table) it could not be of very great use or importance.

The other six old gentlemen, members of the Unit, all of them by now well into their seventies or eighties, were not particularly sorry to be offered compulsory retirement and permitted to make their way severally to Arizona, Tibet, Patagonia, the Pyrenees, Tasmania, and an Irish mountain called SlieveLeague, where they had been nursing future retirement homes for many years past; and the room where they had been accustomed to gather in Fort Pilgrim stood empty and silent – though no more silent, to be sure, than it had for many days in the past, as the aged seers sat meditating and concentrating over the map. 'Remote sensing' had at one time commanded a budget of $1.1 million – that was just after Warren Wilmslow, the kidnapped State Department official had been located in a cave in the Atlas Mountains. But now the closure rated no more than a small paragraph in the local paper. And the furniture in the empty room might have remained gathering dust for years to come, had not the news story caught the eye of an old lady in Washington, and also that of a gang boss in Detroit.

The old lady, Miss Letitia O'Brien, had for many years run a curio and second-hand furniture store called Rattletrap Corner. In her store might be found Sheraton and Chippendale furniture, Dresden china, Crown Derby, treasures of Chinese jade and Fabergé, silk patchwork quilts of inestimable value quietly rotting away besides immense accumulations of dusty and probably worthless rubbish. Over the years the stock had piled higher and higher until at last there was only one small corner of space left clear in the five rooms that made up the store. Miss O'Brien declared that, as soon as this last space was filled, she would have all her stock packed and crated and despatched to her family home at Castle Knocka in Ireland.

'For it's homesick I am, and weary of the tedious world of bustle and commerce here in Washington D.C., and there's my sister Lydia a-wearying and a-waiting for me, and I wearying for her to the same degree; and the castle standing empty and desolate all this while that might as well be filled with those same collectables that I have collected; and I have heard that every Irish dairymaid these days is so rich she can afford Carrickmacross lace for her cap-trimmings, and the land overrun with tourists from Easter Eve to Saint Lucy's day, so there's a fortune waiting to be made from the bed and breakfasts'.

From which it might be inferred that some time had elapsed since Miss O'Brien had visited her native isle, since very few dairymaids in Ireland now wear caps, lace-trimmed or otherwise.

The news item about the closure of the Psychovisuals Unit interested her particularly, since for many years Miss O'Brien had been a close friend of Nelson Far-eye.

'Indeed it's a grievous loss to the world that the dear man is out of it. But – who knows? – maybe his far-eye is watching all manner of things, this very day, in distant realms that even he could not have penetrated before – just think of that! And now that grand old chair of his, the office chair that he sat in, year in, year out, a-harkening and a-looking – that chair must be just infused with his insights, buzzing with his brain-waves, pulsing with the man's very heartbeats – that chair must be worth a life's experience, I'll be bound, to the next human soul that sits in it! Just imagine it! Wouldn't that same chair be worth having?'

Oddly enough, the leader of the Condors gang in Detroit, a tall, thin, evil man called Dodington Sneyd, had been smitten with precisely the same notion. Sneyd was a convinced believer in telepathy and presentiments, which had several times been turned to most satisfactory account in Condor gang operations, where precision and hair-trigger timing were of vital importance.

'You go and get hold of Nelson's chair,' he ordered his Number Two, Crash Corby. 'I've got a notion that the guy that sits next in that chair, if he can only get on to Nelson Far-eye's wavelength – why, I reckon he could soak up enough information to blackmail the whole *world*! Just fancy being able to predict what'll blow up next – volcanoes, decaying nuclear power plants, fault-lines, earthquakes – very likely weather changes, hurricanes, tidal waves –'

'Would he be able to *set off* eruptions or hurricanes?' wondered Crash Corby, who was valued for his fidelity, not for his brain-power. 'Could Nelson Far-eye do that?'

'Who the hell knows what he could do? Don't stand there gabbing, you get after that chair!' snapped Dodington Sneyd. 'Take a plane to Washington D.C., find out who deals with selling off used government furniture, make an offer, bring the stuff back! Fifty dollars should cover the whole roomful.'

Unfortunately for the Condor gang, Miss O'Brien had nipped in with her offer already. In fact she acquired the seven chairs for ten dollars (the Library of Congress had put in a prior claim for the map table).

Crash Corby therefore arrived next day at a dusty street corner in a shabby, leafy Washington suburb just in time to see the seven chairs, which had been ranged in a melancholy row on the sidewalk outside Miss O'Brien's store, being loaded into a huge furniture removal container; and they were followed, with surprisingly efficient speed, by desks, spinets, beds, tapestry, trunks, wardrobes, and easels.

Corby might just have had time to grab one of the chairs. But how to be sure which was the right one? To him they all looked exactly alike. As, indeed, they were: dusty old office chairs, made of wood, from the long-ago days when plastic was for toothbrushes.

'Where's that lot going?' Corby asked a man hoisting a piano, who had the legend POTOMAC PICK-UP inscribed across his baseball cap.

'Galway. Container ship down the river,' said the man, and jerked his head in that direction, as he nestled the piano into a snug corner of the container.

'Galway. Where's that?'

'Ireland.'

When Crash Corby returned, chairless and forlorn, to his boss in Detroit with this information, Sneyd was justifiably annoyed.

'Why didn't you get the address they were going to?' he rasped.

Luckily Miss O'Brien had left a forwarding address, Knocka Castle, Galway, for business mail arriving at Rattletrap Corner after her departure. This was elicited by telephone, and, three days later, the two representatives of the Condor gang found themselves, fur-coated and shivering, climbing out of their rented car in the centre of a huge, misty, moist Irish plain, to survey a crenellated, battlemented pile of damp grey stone, with gothic windows and four separate circular towers, ivy-grown, crumbling, apparently deserted, and in a very poor state of repair.

A brand-new sign, however, by the ruinous gate said: 'This Property recently acquired by the Historic Legacy Trust. No plants, stones, woodwork, or art contents to be tampered with or removed.'

Another sign, in the centre of the large moss-grown lawn in front of the building, which was scattered with broken and rotting timbers from the roof and overgrown with a fine population of toadstools, said: 'THIS IS A NO-GO AREA! This lawn *must not be walked on*. It contains seven different species of Red Data fungus which are on the Protected lists of nine different European countries.'

'My, oh my,' said Corby who, descended from Italian forebears, enjoyed a dish of pasta with fungi. 'I guess we came to the right spot.'

'But where's all the folk?' demanded Dodington Sneyd, annoyed. 'Why aren't the movers here, unloading all the furnishings?'

Beyond the moss-grown lawn, with its precious load of Hygophorus and Tricholobia stretched a wide, flat, greyish-green expanse, dissolving far away into distant mists; it looked like pasture land, except that no beasts grazed on it; in fact it was swamp, also under a preservation order, for it nurtured a great many rare marsh plants and formed a haven for rare divers and water birds; it was known locally as Black Feakle's Slough.

The two Condors found a wrinkled native half a mile away and questioned him.

'Ah, sure, it'll be another month, I'd say, sirs, before Miss Lydia looks to see the chattels roll up to her doorstep – with the slowness of the ocean transport that's in it these days,' he told the gentlemen. 'Miss Lydia's there, habiting in the castle, bless ye, but she don't trouble herself to come out for visitors, not a great deal, any more. Her quarters is round at the back, if ye wish to see the lady, and ye must keep a careful watch for Bran, as the dog's a holy terror. When the furnishings are delivered ye'll see Miss Lydia emerge fast enough, yes indeed.'

'Does that mean that we have to stay here for a month?' said Corby, looking round him with great disfavour at the huge green emptiness of Galway. The drizzle fell. The wind whuffled at their ears. Overhead a towering grey sky moved slowly past.

'We'd best stop in the nearest town,' said Dodington Sneyd.

That, the wrinkled native told them, was Ballycrumble, a mere twenty foggy miles to the west.

'Even Nelson Far-eye couldn't see across *this* country,' muttered Corby.

Re-passing the castle, they halted and picked their way along a path to the rear, where they found some dejected hens and a vegetable garden.

'What a dump,' said Sneyd disgustedly. 'What a tip. And it's been acquired by the Historic Legacy Trust – what for, in Pete's name? It looks like something that got left behind when Noah was packing up the Ark –'

'And how can I be of help to you two gentlemen?' inquired a polite, silvery voice.

Corby had seen the elderly Miss Letitia O'Brien in Washington, directing the movers' men who were crating up her furniture. This sister, Miss Lydia, was perhaps ten or twelve years older, thin and brittle as a sprig of dried parsley. She wore faded jeans, had a thatch of scanty, smooth, snow-white hair and two piercing blue eyes that looked calmly out from a crow's-nest of wrinkles.

The calm was quite comprehensible, for her question was accompanied by a continuo of low, grinding growl, like a distant motor starting up, and she greeted the visitors with her hand on the head of a massive hound, part wolfhound, part Dobermann, who stood limberly beside her and eyed the strangers in a thoughtful manner, as if he were judging where, if needful, would be the best point in them to sink his teeth.

'Miss O'Brien?' said Sneyd hastily. 'We – we are friends of your sister –'

'Indeed? Is that so now? I have just been speaking with her on the telephone – she is at Shannon Airport – I'm bound to tell ye she said nothing of friends coming this way.'

Sneyd was annoyed. When caught out in a lie, his first recourse was generally to shoot somebody dead, and his hand moved to the gun under his fur coat. But Corby, for once, was quicker than his chief to size up a situation. Miss O'Brien would not be much use to them shot. It would be far better to acquire some information from her first.

'Ma'am, we met your sister in Washington D.C. when she was crating up the bits and pieces from her store to send over here. There were seven chairs in the load that –'

'That we have an interest in acquiring,' completed Sneyd smoothly. The hand moved away from the gun again.

'Ah, so. Seven chairs.'

'But they were all packed up, you see, when we arrived at the store. So – so – as we were too late there –'

'So we'd like to put in a bid for them this side of the water,' Sneyd finished.

'Seven chairs.'

Distant thunder. The dog rumbling again.

'The astrologer's chair,' said Miss Lydia.

'Ma'am?'

'From the Department of Government Psychics that closed down. Am I right? Letty said she had bought them. Nelson Far-eye's chair? Is that it?'

'Ma'am –'

'What do you intend to do with the chair?' Miss O'Brien inquired.

'Lady, that's no business of yours,' said Sneyd shortly.

'No? There I can't agree with you. The chair is my sister's property at present. We – she and I – are very keenly concerned with our surroundings, with the future of Tellus.'

'Tellus? Tellus what?' Now even Sneyd was at a loss.

'The globe that we live on. My sister's friend Nelson Far-eye possessed such a remarkable view of the future, and of the disposition of natural resources around our planet – as well as *un*-natural resources, for the matter of that – we should not like to see anything that appertained to him passing into the wrong hands –'

'Oh, but there's no chance of that, Ma'am –' began Corby eagerly. 'No, no indeed! My friend here – who has psychic powers as good as that of Dr Far-eye – my friend has a great wish to sit on that chair – just for the experience, you know, Ma'am? Just to pick up a few vibes!' Ignoring Sneyd's frightful scowl, he went on hopefully, 'Just when do you expect your sister, Miss Lydia? And – and the things?'

'My sister will be here in an hour or two. The furniture –' Miss Lydia fixed her two uninvited guests with a chill blue eye – 'the furniture not for several weeks. And there is no question of our selling any articles. I cannot promise that my sister will have the least interest in your proposals. I can only suggest that, if you feel it is worth the bother, you find yourselves accommodation in Ballycrumble and return here at the end of that time. If you feel you must pursue this. But I assure you, it is hopeless. *Good* afternoon to you. Bran – see the gentlemen to their car.'

Bran, with another terrifying rumble, did so.

At The Fisherman's Rest hotel in Ballycrumble, Sneyd and Corby learned more about the two ladies who owned Castle Knocka.

'Sure, 'tis a museum Miss Lydia plans to make of it – a Museum of the Earth, if you please! People's common life from all over the globe. Grants of money from hither and thither, the ladies have procured, if you will believe me – and now they plan to repair the structure and furnish it with all Miss Letty's bits and sticks. 'Twill be open to the public in five years' time, and a rare benefit to the neighbourhood. And the croquet lawn classified as Ancient Grassland, God save the mark. There's fungi on it, ye see, that cannot abide nitrogen and, it seems, the soil there at Knocka is entirely to their taste – 'tis said that, if there was any damage to that same turf it would take fifty years to put it to rights again. Fifty years! Can you credit that? Ah, they're a fine pair, Miss Lyddy and Miss Letty – tough as whaleskin and sharp as diamonds, the pair of them!'

'Why don't we just blow up the old biddies and the castle together before the furniture gets here?' suggested Corby in their large, icy-cold bedroom at The Fishermen's Rest, but Sneyd shook his head.

'That might upset the vibes. We got to play this cool and careful. We'll wait till the load's delivered and *then* make our approach; in a place like this, where you can hear someone open a coke can at the other end of town, we're sure to get plenty of warning when the ship docks at Galway.'

Sure enough, two weeks later, word spread over the countryside that five huge container trucks, loaded with furniture and household goods, were making their careful way eastwards from the port of Galway. Their rate of progress was slow and easy, not more than thirty miles a day.

''Tis the way they received instructions to be gentle and harmonious with the articles,' people explained to each other. 'There's a grand deal of historic treasures in there, never forgetting the mystical seat of Nelson Far-eye, God rest him.'

For word concerning this remarkable piece of furniture had also percolated over the countryside, and quite a large crowd of interested spectators with nothing better to do had begun to assemble and to accompany the convoy, mounted on bicycles, donkeys, farm carts, racehorses in training and roller-skates.

'Good grief!' said Dodington Sneyd disgustedly, as the two Condors presently pulled up at Castle Knocka, having timed their arrival a little in advance of the furniture convoy. 'It's like a flaming three-ring circus. Donnybrook Fair on wheels.'

'I daresay they don't get much entertainment locally,' observed Corby, looking at the crowds. 'A museum will certainly brighten things up round here.'

The two O'Brien sisters were waiting, stately as frosted cobwebs, on the castle doorstep.

Sneyd went to hold converse with them, when the trucks were still half a mile away across the flat landscape. The dog Bran eyed him thoughtfully but remained quiet; there were too many people about to start chewing up a single visitor. But he let out a low growl, just as a reminder. Sneyd thoughtfully stroked the butt of the machine pistol hidden under his fur coat.

'Good morning, ladies.'

''Tis the fellow who was wishing to make an offer for Nelson's chair,' said Lydia to her sister.

Letitia shook her silvery head.

'Away with you, sirs! Away! Didn't my sister give you the only answer you'll be having from us? And what use is it at all for you to be lingering here? That chair's not for sale; indeed, 'tis the key to the whole collection.'

Sneyd mentioned a sum of money; then, as this did not seem to impress the sisters at all, he quadrupled it.

Miss Letitia looked at him wearily. 'Away with you,' she said again. 'Devil a bit of use is it your stravaguing here at this while's time – you'll get no other answer.'

'Listen, lady,' said Sneyd, holding tight on to his patience. 'If I can't buy it from you – will you just let me *sit* in the chair? For a couple of minutes – say five minutes? I'll pay the same –'

Both sisters eyed him as carefully as if they were in the marketplace inspecting a doubtful joint of meat. Both shook their heads.

'I'd pay you enough – just for that – to put this whole crumbling mess of a castle in order,' shouted Sneyd.

'Sir: your money's of no interest to us. What *does* occupy us –' the sisters looked at one another and both nodded thoughtfully – 'is the nasty blackguardly explosive aura that you carry wrapped around you like a red shroud – faith, it's worse than a whiff of poison gas! And *that's* what we don't want brought anywhere close to Nelson's chair – amn't I right, Lyddy?'

''Deed and you are, sister,' nodded Lydia. 'It would be worse than dropping a bomb on a bird's nest. The whole future of the globe might be deranged.'

Sneyd threw them a furious look, and again his hand caressed the butt of the gun. But their attention had left him, for now the first of the lorries had rolled to a halt in the wide, weedy castle driveway.

It was an open vehicle, perhaps a cattle truck at other times, and in it could be seen what the transporters had evidently reckoned to be the least important part of the load, goods and furnishings that would take no hurt from a bit of fresh, moist Irish weather, and needed the least care in packing and handling. Indeed, two of the drivers – there were three allotted to each truck – were to be seen taking their ease on top of the load, one fast asleep on an old truckle-bedstead, the other stretched out blissfully on seven wooden chairs which had been lashed together side by side.

However, as soon as the truck came to a halt, both men sprang up alertly, unshipped a crane which was attached to the driver's cab at the back, clinched its hook firmly into the rope that fastened the seven chairs together, and swung them out of the truck, landing them with elegant precision exactly in the centre of the moss-grown lawn that was designated as Ancient Grassland.

A cheer went up from the assembled spectators.

The two Misses O'Brien bustled down to greet the truck.

Miss Letitia looked carefully at the seven chairs on the lawn.

'That's a grand job you have done there, my men,' she said. 'But we'll have no more articles on the lawn, *if* you please! The chairs may stay there. In fact that's the very place for them. I couldn't have planned it better myself. But for the rest of the articles – on the drive, here, if you will be so good. No one – *nobody* – is to set foot on that grass.'

The men nodded, beamed, hoisted out a wardrobe, and dropped it on the weedy gravel.

But meanwhile Corby had Sneyd by the arm and was hissing in his ear.

'*Those are the chairs.* Those very ones there, on the grass!'

A look of supreme satisfaction spread over Sneyd's face.

'*Great!* I'll be out there and settled on them before they can –'

He started for the grass pitch. But Miss Letitia had her eye on him, and so had the dog Bran. With a howl worthy of a werewolf, Bran streaked in pursuit and grabbed at the flying skirts of Sneyd's fur coat.

Sneyd spun round and shot the dog.

'Anyone else tries to stop me, I'll shoot them too!' he yelled, and set one foot on the grass.

'Pick him up – you, with the crane – pick him up!' directed Miss Lydia.

The crane operator swung his hook over, snatching up Sneyd by the belt of his coat. The gun flew out of his hand and spun on to the grass.

'What'll I do with him now, Ma'am?' asked the operator.

'Toss him over there.' The old lady gestured with her umbrella.

Like a bird with a worm or a cat with a mouse the crane flung its dangling prey beyond the border of the mossy lawn, over the low stone parapet, and far into the green, flat, shiny expanse which was known by the locals as Black Feakle's Slough.

Dodington Sneyd sank into it and was seen no more.

Corby, shocked and startled to the marrow at the horrid suddenness of his boss's fate, wasted no more time, but beat a strategic retreat to the rental car, pointed it hastily in the direction of Shannon Airport, and drove away at top speed.

'That's the last we'll see of those fellows, I'd say,' remarked Miss Lydia with satisfaction. 'Now – if all you friends will turn a hand to unloading the trucks, we'll soon have the castle furnished. Only, let nobody set foot on the grass plat.'

'What about them chairs, Miss Lyddy? Are they to remain there for a while's time?'

'For ever,' said Miss Lydia. 'That's the best place for them. And the gun likewise, till it rusts away.'

With great goodwill the spectators of this interesting event turned to, and unloaded all the contents of the trucks, until the last mat, coal scuttle, teaspoon, and napkin ring was inside Castle Knocka.

Then they assembled in the castle kitchen for slices of hot barm brack and tea, generously laced with drams from the castle cellar.

''Tis a fortunate thing they have no breathalysers on the road betwixt here and Galway Bay,' said one of the drivers to his mate. 'And it's your turn to drive now, Mickey, for you slept all the way here.'

Mickey, a fat, serene man, smiled blissfully.

'Indeed and I did, and the best sleep it was I've had these fifty three years! And wasn't I dreaming the grandest dream all the way from Galway to here, stretched out on thim chairs.'

'What was the dream about?' inquired Miss Lydia, handing him a slice of toasted brack.

'Seven ways to save the world, Ma'am! Seven ways to save the world!'

The Beastman of Ballyloch

Michael Morpurgo

Illustrated by Christian Birmingham

THERE WAS once an ogre so pitted and crumpled in his face, so twisted in his body, that no one could bear even to look at him. He was known in all the country around as 'the Beastman of Ballyloch'. He lived by himself on a small island in the middle of a great dark lake. Being left on his own as a small child, as he had been when his mother died, and shunned ever since by all humankind, he had never learned to speak as other men do, so that when he tried he sounded like a cawing croaking crow, and no words came out.

Lonely though he was on his island, he was never completely alone, for with him lived all the wild things he loved so well – the squirrels, the otters, the herons and the moorhens. But of all the creatures that lived with him on the island, it was the swans he loved best. He mended their broken wings, untangled them from fishing twine and drove the marauding gulls away from their nests. For the swans, the island was a safe haven. They knew the ogre was not like the people who lived across the lake in the village of Ballyloch. He would not hunt them or steal their eggs, or throw sticks at them. To them, he was not at all, not at all hideous. He was their guardian and the kindest man that ever lived, a trusted friend.

He lived simply in the log cabin he had built for himself, under a roof he had thatched himself. Under the thatch it was cool enough in the summer months, and just so long as he kept the fire going, warm enough in the winter too. He grew all the corn he needed in his one-acre field, and all the vegetables he could want in the sheltered garden behind the log cabin. When the fish were rising of an evening in the great dark lake, then he would often go out in his boat and catch himself a fine fat fish for his supper – seatrout perhaps, or brown trout, or even better a silver salmon fresh up from the sea. The ogre needed to eat well, for he was half as big again as any man in Ballyloch.

Much as the people of Ballyloch hated the sight of the ogre, they needed him, for he was the best thatcher for miles around and they knew it. He was also the cheapest. All he asked in payment for a day's work was a wheelbarrowload of peat for his fire. So whenever there was a barn or a house to be rethatched, he would set out across the lake in his boat, and he would always be escorted by a flotilla of swans. The villagers would see him coming, and the cry would go up. 'The Beastman is coming! The Beastman is coming!' Many of the children would be hustled away indoors as he tied up his boat by the quayside, as he came limping up the village street. Others, the older ones more often, would laugh and jeer at him, throw stones at him even; and then run off screaming up the alleyways. He did not blame them. He had ears. He knew well enough what they had all been told: 'Don't you ever go near the Beastman. And don't ever set foot on his island either. If you do he'll gobble you up.'

In spite of this, the ogre did his best to smile at everyone. He would always wave cheerily; but not one of them would ever wave back nor greet him kindly. The ogre endured all the averted eyes, all the wicked whisperings, all the children's taunts because he loved to be amongst his own, to hear the sound of human voices, to see the people at their work, the children at their play, to feel that he was once more a man amongst men. From high up on a rooftop, as he drove in his spars or combed his thatch, he could look down over the village and watch them all going about their lives. That was as close as he was ever going to get to them. He knew he could hope for nothing more. In all his life he had never once been invited into their houses, never once warmed himself at their hearths. He would do his day's thatching, wheel his barrowload of peat down to the quayside in the evening, load his boat and row back to his island across the great dark lake, his beloved swans swimming alongside.

It was a summer's day and there was a fresh run of seatrout in the lake. Dozens of fishing boats had come out from Ballyloch, and the sound of happy children rippled across the water. The ogre sat on the grassy bank of his island and watched them. He thought at first it was the sound of flying swans, their wings singing in the air; but then he saw her, a young woman in a straw hat. It was she who was singing. She was standing up in her boat and hauling in her line. Her boat was close to the island, closer to the shore than they usually came, much closer than all the other boats. How the ogre's heart soared as he listened. Nothing was ever as sweet as this.

There was a sudden shriek and a splash, and the boat was empty and rocking violently. The straw hat was floating on the water, but of the young woman there was no sign at all. The ogre did not stop even to take off his boots and his jacket. He dived straight into the icy water and swam out towards the boat. He saw her come up once, her hands clutching at the air before she sank again. She came up a second time, gasping for life and was gone again almost at once. The ogre went down after her, caught her round the waist and brought her to the surface. He swam her back to the island and laid her down in the grass. She lay there, limp and lifeless, not a movement, not a breath. The ogre called and called to her, but she would not wake. He held his head in his hands and wept out loud.

'Why are you crying?' She was speaking! The ogre took his hands away. She was sitting up! 'You're the Beastman, aren't you?' she went on, shrinking from him. She looked around her. 'I'm on the island, aren't I? I shouldn't be here. I shouldn't be talking to you.' For a few moments she stared at him and said nothing. 'It must have been you that saved me. You pulled me out!' The ogre thought of speaking, but dared not. The sound of his croaking voice would only make him more fearsome, more repellent. The girl was suddenly smiling at him. 'You did, didn't you? You saved my life. But why? After all I did to you. When I was a child I used to throw stones at you, do you know that? I used to laugh at you. And now you've saved my life.'

The ogre had to speak, had to tell her none of that mattered, had to tell her how beautifully she sang. He tried, but of course all that came out was a crow's croak. 'All right,' she went on. 'Maybe you can't speak words, but you can speak. And you can hear me, can't you? My father – you know my father. He's the weaver, you thatched our house once when I was little, remember? – he always told me you were deaf and dumb. But you're not, are you? He said you were mad too, that you gobble up children for your tea. But you're not like that at all. I know it from your eyes you're not. How can I ever thank you? I have nothing to give you. I am not rich. I know, I know. Shall I teach you how to speak words? Shall I? First I shall teach you my name – Miranda. Miranda. You will say it. You will.' The ogre took her small hands in his and wept again, but this time for sheer joy. 'And I'm going to tell everyone what you did, and they won't ever believe any more all the terrible things they've heard about you.' She shivered suddenly. 'I'm cold,' she said.

The ogre carried her into his cabin, set her down close to the fire, and wrapped her in his best blanket. He hung out her clothes to dry and gave her a bowl of piping hot leek and potato soup. Afterwards, warmed through inside and out, Miranda slept for a while; and the ogre sat and

watched her, happier than he had been in his whole life.

By the time she woke, her clothes were dry again, and he rowed her back across the lake, towing her own boat behind them. She talked to him all the while, and that was when she told him of the smiling stranger with the pointed teeth who had just come to lodge in the village. 'No one knows where he comes from, but Father says he'll make us all rich. That's what everyone says. He may too, but I don't think so. There's something shifty about him. He smiles too much. Father says he'd make me a good husband. I tell you, I'd rather marry a billygoat. Him and his magic Stardust! "What do you most want in all the world?" he says. Well, of course, everyone says the same thing, don't they?: "We want to be rich."'

The ogre had stopped rowing, leaving the boat drifting towards the quay. 'Stardust. Stardust.' The word rang in his head like a warning bell. '"All you have to do is sprinkle my Stardust on your cornfields," says the smiling stranger,' she went on, '"and your corn will grow faster in a week than in a whole year. Sprinkle Stardust on the lake and before the week's out you'll be catching fish as big as whales." All we have to do is buy his silly Stardust.'

At this the ogre became suddenly very agitated, croaking and cawing as if wracked inside by some terrible pain. She tried to understand him. She tried to calm him. She wasn't to know the terrible story echoing now in his head, how his mother had told him on her deathbed of the smiling stranger with the pointed teeth who had come to their house just before he was born, and asked her exactly the same question: 'What do you most want in all the world?' 'A boy child who will grow big and strong,' she had said. And she'd paid him all her life savings. 'Sprinkle this magic Stardust on your supper tonight, and you shall have your wish,' the smiling stranger had said, and he'd taken the money and ridden away on his fine horse. Only weeks later his mother had given birth to a baby boy, bigger and stronger than any man child ever born, but ugly as sin and as misshapen as it is possible to be, and with a voice that croaked like a crow.

The ogre reached forward and clasped Miranda's hands, striving all he could to say the words to warn her, but they would not come. 'Don't worry,' she told him. 'I shall come back. I promised to teach you to speak, didn't I? And I shall. I will come tomorrow. Tomorrow I shall teach you my name. I promise. I promise.'

As the boat touched the quay she leaped out and ran away. Suddenly she stopped and turned to him, her hand on her head. 'My straw hat. I think I've lost my straw hat. But why am I complaining about a silly hat when I have my life? Thank you, thank you for my life.' And the ogre watched her go, his heart crying out after her, until he could see her no more in the gathering dusk.

That evening, as the ogre sat alone and wretched in his log cabin, the people of Ballyloch gathered in their hall to hear the smiling stranger with the pointed teeth tell them how everyone of them could be ten, twenty times as rich, a hundred times as rich inside a week. 'Sprinkle this magic Stardust,' he declared, 'and you will harvest gold.' They all listened in silence, and wondered and believed; but Miranda was not there to hear it.

Nothing ever happened in Ballyloch without the whole world knowing it. She had been seen coming back from the island with the ogre. As soon as she got home her father had sent her to her room and locked her in. Through the door she had tried to tell him how the ogre had rescued her from drowning, how he was kind and gentle and not at all as everyone said he was. She begged him to let her go back to the island the next day so that she could fulfil her promise and teach him how to speak.

'Never,' thundered her father. 'Promise me you will never go back there, or you will stay in your room till you do, d'you hear me?' But Miranda would promise no such thing.

So she was not there to protest when the villagers bought their sacks of

Stardust from the smiling stranger with the pointed teeth. But she *was* watching from her window the next morning as they sprinkled their Stardust all over their cornfields, and out onto the great dark lake. From his island the ogre saw it too, and hung his head in despair. Somehow he had to warn Miranda when she came. Somehow he had to make her understand. All day he sat and watched and waited for her boat, but no boat came anywhere near his island. By nightfall Miranda had still not come.

All night long he sat there, all the next day, all the next week. Still she did not come and she did not come. On the seventh day, cries of delight echoed across the water as the villagers hauled gigantic fish out of the lake, fish so huge they could scarcely drag them into their boats. And the ogre could see clearly enough from the island that the corn in the fields was already twice the height it had been the week before. On the seventh night the ogre sat by the lakeside and listened to the sound of revelry wafting over the still dark water. He knew it for certain now. There was no hope. She would never come back to him. Those eyes of hers which had promised so much would, like the smiling stranger's magic Stardust, bring nothing but pain.

Distant thunder sounded through the mountains, heralding a storm; but still the ogre did not seek the shelter of his cabin. When the lightening crackled and crashed overhead, he did not move. He wished only that it would strike him dead. When the cold rain lashed down on him and the wind howled across the lake and chilled him to the bone, he sat where he was and prayed he would freeze to death so that he would not have to face the morning.

Morning came though, and he found himself numb all over but still alive. The storm had passed by. The morning sun broke through the mist and warmed him. Beside him the swans slept, heads tucked under their wings. That was when the ogre first heard the wailing from across the water. Everyone in the village was out in the streets and gazing up at their houses. Every roof in the village had been ripped off and the thatch strewn about the streets. Out in the cornfields there was no corn left standing. Everywhere the people stood dazed and weeping. Many of them were down at the water's edge and looking out over the lake in stunned horror.

Only then did the ogre notice it himself. The lake was no longer dark. It was green, an unnatural green such as he had never seen before. He knelt down by the lakeside and ran his hand through the water. It wasn't the water that was green. It was covered on the surface by a thick layer of slime. Further out, a moorhen bobbed about in it, green all over. She tried to take off, tried to fly, but could not. An otter ran along the shore, not black and glistening as he usually was, but entirely green from head to tail. And fish lay dead in the water, on the shore, everywhere the ogre looked.

The swans were gliding out through it, dipping their long and lovely necks. He shouted at them to come back, but it was too late. As they washed and preened themselves, every one of them was turning green, and already some of them were choking. He ran to the end of the island to see if the lake was green all around. It was, as far as the eye could see. A solitary duck quacked from in amongst the reeds. She tried to fly, but her feathers were matted and heavy with slime. The ogre knew she was never going to fly again.

As he watched her struggling in vain to clean herself, the ogre noticed Miranda's straw hat floating in amongst the reeds, and around it the only clear dark water in the entire lake. He waded out and picked it up. One look underneath the dripping hat and his heart surged with sudden hope. All his years of thatching told him it was possible. Miranda's hat proved it. But the lake was dying all around him. Not a fish would be left alive, and he knew that unless he could save them in time, all his beloved swans would die too.

He rowed out over the green lake, and as he rowed he saw dead fish floating all around him, bloated on the water. A drowned cormorant drifted by and a heron aarked in terror from the shore, flapping his great wings in a frantic effort to rid himself of the cloying green cloak that would not let him fly. For once the people of Ballyloch paid him little attention as the ogre walked amongst them. They were too busy bemoaning their disaster.

'We brought it on ourselves,' one was saying. 'How were we to know?' said another. 'The stranger promised we'd be rich, and look what ruin he has brought on us instead.' 'We will have no corn to harvest. There will be no fish to catch. We will all starve, all of us.' 'What have we done to deserve this? What have we done?'

The ogre left them and hurried straight to the weaver's house. From her window, Miranda saw him coming and called down to him. 'I tried to come, I tried, but Father forbad me from ever seeing you again. He made me promise I would never go to the island, and when I refused, he shut me in here. I have not been allowed out of my room for a week. And look what has happened in that week. It was the stranger's magic Stardust that did this, I know it was.'

The ogre waved her straw hat in the air, and tried all he could to tell her what he had discovered, but she could make no sense of all his frantic cawing and croaking. 'Just come up and let me out, and then you can tell me. But hurry, hurry, before Father comes back.' The ogre let himself in at the front door and climbed the stairs to Miranda's room. Once the door was unlocked, she took him by the hand and they ran out into the weaving shed where they could be alone and unseen. There, with the roof open to the skies, and the thatch strewn all around their feet, the ogre showed her the straw hat and explained to her as best he could what had to be done to save the lake, and the fish, and the swans, and the people of

Ballyloch too. When he had finished, she reached up and touched his face tenderly. 'You are no Beastman,' she said. 'You are the *Bestman*, the best man in Ballyloch, the best man in all the world.'

When the people heard the churchbell ringing out, they gathered in the village, believing it was the mayor who had called them together. But the mayor was as puzzled as everyone else when out of the church came Miranda, her straw hat in her hand, and looming behind her the huge form of Beastman of Ballyloch. Her father was spluttering in his fury, but before he could find the words to protest, Miranda began:

'The fish cannot breathe and the birds cannot fly,' she said. 'The lake is poisoned. If it cannot be saved, then we, too, will die with it. Like the otters, like the herons, we cannot live without our fish.'

'Why is the Beastman here?' cried her father, pushing through the crowd. 'I told you to keep away from him.'

'Get him away. We don't want him near the children,' said the mayor. 'Send him back to his island. We don't need him.'

'And who will thatch our roofs if he does not?' Miranda was angry now, angrier than she had ever been, and they heard it in her voice. No one could answer her. No one dared answer her, not even her father. She spoke only softly, but everyone listened. 'I'm telling you, we need him for more than thatching, too. He has come to save the lake, and he is the only one among us who can. He can't tell you how, because he can't speak as we do. So, for now, I shall speak for him.'

She held up her straw hat for everyone to see. 'Only a few days ago, this man, this ogre, this "Beastman" as we call him, saved me from drowning. He didn't gobble me up, he saved my life. I was wearing this hat when I fell in and I thought it was lost. He found it this morning in the lake, and he saw that all around it the water was clear. Look underneath, and you will see how it soaks up the green slime that is choking the life out of our lake. His idea is that we should weave, all of us together, a huge straw carpet and lay it out on the lake. We shall weave it with flax – Father has enough flax in his weaving sheds to do it. I shall teach you all how to weave. It can be done. It must be done. We have all the straw we need, all the corn broken by the storm, all the thatch lying loose in the streets. Once the carpet is made, we shall tow it out and leave it on the lake to soak up the green slime.'

They stood, mouths agape. No one spoke a word. 'We must have the carpet on the lake by nightfall,' Miranda went on. 'We may be too late already to save all the fish, and all the birds; but we may still save most of them if we hurry. We may even save ourselves.'

No one argued, not even her father. Soon every man, woman and child was out gathering the strewn thatch and the battered corn, and spreading it out to be woven into a great straw carpet. All day they toiled, Miranda and the ogre amongst them. For the very first time in his life the ogre felt the warmth of their smiles. No one stopped for a moment, not for food, not for drink. They worked till their backs ached, till their hands were raw, until the carpet of straw was woven together at last. When they had finished, it stretched along the lakeside from one end of the village to the other. At dusk, towed by twenty fishing boats, they hauled it out onto the lake and left it floating there. Neither the ogre nor Miranda nor anyone could do any more. Now the straw had to be left to work its magic. How the people of Ballyloch prayed that night that the straw magic would be stronger than the Stardust magic of the smiling stranger. How they prayed that their lake could be saved.

When the ogre rowed home to his island that night, Miranda was with him. Time and again they stopped to scoop half-drowned birds from the slime, so that by the time they reached the island, the bottom of the boat was filled with them, all struggling for life. Once inside his cabin, they cleaned them off as best they could with straw wisps and clean water, and then they set about bringing in all the surviving swans they could find.

They, too, had to be cleaned off and washed down, until their feathers were white again and gleaming in the firelight.

All night, as they worked together, Miranda was teaching him. Tired as he was, he was determined to be able to say at least one word by morning. Over and over again he practised 'Miranda'; and by morning he could say 'Manda', which, she said, was as good, if not better, than Miranda anyway. It was a start. There would be many more nights, she said, and many more words.

Both were dreading the coming of dawn, for the glow of love was over them, and like all lovers they wanted time to stand still. But in the back of their minds, too, was the awful fear that the green slime would still be there in the morning, that the straw carpet might have failed them. Exhausted by now, they fell asleep by the fire, the swans all around them.

They were woken by the sound of cheering, and ran outside. Every boat in the village, it seemed, was heading towards the island, and the lake was dancing with the early morning sun. The straw magic had worked! There were still some patches of green close to the shore, but they were few and far between. There would be enough clear water now for the fish to breathe, for the birds to wash themselves clean. The people of Ballyloch leapt out onto the grassy bank, hoisted the ogre and Miranda onto their shoulders and carried them off in triumph around the island. Above them flew the swans, their wings singing in the air.

Set down at last on their feet again, Miranda kissed away in one minute all the sadness the ogre had stored up inside him all his life. 'This is my man,' she declared joyously. 'This is the *Bestman* of Ballyloch.' And there was not a soul there who disagreed. 'And who,' she asked him, 'who is the best girl in Ballyloch?'

'Manda,' said the Bestman of Ballyloch. 'Manda. Manda.'

By the time they married a few months later, he could say the name of everyone who lived in Ballyloch, and could tell Miranda what every bird he saw was called, and every animal too come to that. After that he very soon learnt to talk well enough to make himself understood. Of course his work was more in demand than ever after the storm damage. Now wherever he went, he was invited in to eat at their tables and to warm himself at their hearths.

He was mending the roof on the weaving shed when Miranda's father came in carrying over his arm the biggest and the most beautiful jacket he had ever made.

'For you,' he said. 'This is to ask your pardon, and to thank you for saving my daughter, for saving all of us.' The ogre tried it on and it fitted perfectly. 'You do not need to live out on your island any more,' said Miranda's father. 'Come and live with us in the village. You are one of us now.'

'It is kind of you, and this jacket is fit for a prince,' said the ogre. 'But

Manda and I, we must stay with our swans.'

It was sometime later that their first child was born out on the island, a girl child; and she was as healthy and as beautiful as it is possible to be. They were sitting by the fire one evening, the child sleeping in the cradle beside them. The ogre was silent with his own thoughts, thoughts Miranda found she could often guess at just by looking at him. 'She does not know it yet,' he said. 'But when she grows up, she will know I am ugly.'

'You are not ugly,' cried Miranda. 'You are as beautiful as your daughter is beautiful, as beautiful as your swans are beautiful. Do you think I would look twice at some smooth-faced Prince Charming? You're my man, my Bestman, and don't you forget it. I love you, every bulbous bump of you, every craggy crease of you, you great oaf! Now, off with you and catch my supper.'

'Salmon or trout?'

'Trout tonight,' she said. 'I feel like a nice fat brown trout.'

'Well, you don't look like one,' he replied, and he was gone out of the door before she could find anything to throw at him.

Shock Forest

MARGARET MAHY

Illustrated by Robert Ingpen

THE CARMODYS found the red gate easily when they knew exactly what it was they had to look for.

'Just over the hill, and we'll be there,' said Eddie's mother.

'Our own forest!' said Eddie. 'A whole forest! All ours!'

They had inherited something out of a fairy tale. 'A whole forest,' Eddie said again.

'I'm soooo sick of hearing you say that,' groaned Tara. 'Does this look like the gate of a grand old house? Be real!'

It was true Eddie had imagined large iron gates and stone gateposts, rather than this wooden gate sagging on rusty hinges. An avenue of tall gum trees curved away behind the gate. The hillside, running up on the right of the gum trees and running down on the left, was covered in a pelt of hairy brown grass and tussocks.

'Open the gate, Tara,' said their father. 'That'll give you something to do besides grumbling.'

Tara scrambled out and stamped towards the gate, muttering all the way. She had not wanted to leave the city, or her good friends, the shops and the swimming pool. She hated the thought of Shock Forest, and was frightened that her parents might decide, now that her father was out of work, to live there for ever.

'Five hours grumbling! She might get into *The Guinness Book of Records*,' said Eddie.

The car rocked forward, struggling and staggering over hidden ruts in the drive.

'Oh, wow!' cried Tara savagely, delighted to think things might be turning out just as badly as she had always said they would.

The two lines of gum trees came to an end, and the Carmodys bounced up to the top of the slope. Shock Forest lay before them.

The hillside facing them was as brown as all other hills in that part of the world, and almost as empty. Almost – but not quite! Rising among the grass and tussocks were hundreds of blackened fingers, all pointing darkly at the sky.

They were looking at a forest of burned trees, standing like jagged spikes, or lying, black and grey, among the brown grass. Those blackened stumps had been there a long, long time.

'They always called it a forest,' mumbled Mr Carmody at last. 'Shock Forest! It never occurred to me that it was . . . like this.'

'A shock!' said Eddie. 'A real shock!'

'But your father must have known,' said his wife.

'I don't think he did. Well, he never came here,' said Mr Carmody. 'And Mr Caxton never said anything.' Mr Caxton was a young lawyer.

'We have inherited a forest!' cried Tara, copying her father's astonished cry of a fortnight earlier. 'And – hey, Dad – can that dump over there possibly be the great Shock mansion?'

'Well, it's big enough,' said Mr Carmody defensively.

The house sprawled out a hundred metres to their right. It was big, but battered, too, and badly in need of a coat of paint. All the windows looking back towards the forest seemed to be boarded over.

'Oh, well,' said Mrs Carmody, 'a house is a house. And I'm longing for a cup of tea.'

'I thought there would be lawns and gardens,' sighed Eddie, his dreams of grandeur fading. Tussocks marched up to the house and rubbed their tawny heads against its walls.

'The rose gardens and fountains will be on the *other* side,' declared Tara, sounding more and more entertained as things grew worse and worse. 'Just like Shock Forest was going to be on the *other* side of the hill.'

'Oh, shut up, Tara!' said Mr Carmody wearily. 'Give us a break!'

They drove up to the house and stopped at the door.

Mr Carmody turned the large iron key in the lock. The door swung open at once, whining, as if it were afraid of being knocked on, and the Carmodys found themselves in a hall with hooks for coats, and a straight-backed chair with carving on its back and arms. The carpet rustled under their feet. It was covered in dry leaves.

'They must have drifted in under the door,' said Mrs Carmody.

'But where did they drift from?' asked Mr Carmody. 'There isn't a tree in sight. And look! Ashes!'

'We'll sweep it all up tomorrow,' said Mrs Carmody. 'My tongue's hanging out for a cup of tea right now.'

They came into a big room with a fireplace and wide, soft chairs, worn but homely. A huge mantlepiece running above the fireplace was crowded with photographs. In the centre was a picture of a laughing old man, old-fashioned but handsome, and, beside that, the picture of a woman with thick, streaky hair sitting in the very carved chair they had seen in the hall. At one end of the mantlepiece was a stuffed bird . . . a hawk with sad, dusty wings outspread, casting a narrow shadow across the photographs.

'Let's unpack,' said Mr Carmody.

'Unpack! We're not *staying*!' cried Tara. And Eddie realized that she had cheered up a few minutes earlier because she had imagined that, now her parents had *seen* what Shock Forest was actually like, they would naturally go straight home again. Yet, in the end, even Tara was curious

about the house, and helped carry things into the kitchen so she could explore without appearing too interested. Eddie followed her.

It was what people call a farmhouse kitchen, which meant it was as big as most people's dining rooms. An old spade and a worn broom leaned against each other at the back door, and the windows on either side of the door were boarded over. In spite of this, Eddie had the curious feeling that someone was watching them. In a horror film, Great Aunt Isobel would turn out to be sneaking silently up and down secret stairs and spying through hidden peepholes into the lives of other people. As he thought this, Eddie noticed a small hole in the red-boarded wall behind the door – the perfect peephole for a phantom aunt.

That night Eddie lay awake in darkness. The window of his room was boarded over just as the kitchen window had been. But what had Great Aunt Isobel been trying to keep in? Or what had she been trying to keep out? There, in the partly blinded house, Eddie listened to a silence which was not quite silent. Eddie thought he might be hearing the hills breathing, for the sound, if it was a sound, was faint, but vast, too . . . vast, distant and lonely. In the end it sang him to sleep. Yet, once his eyes closed, his eyelids immediately grew transparent, and he looked up through them at an angry red light seething on the ceiling over his bed. And then, as he watched in terror through these glass eyelids, a voice whispered and wept in his ear.

'Burned! It burned,' said the voice. 'It's still burning! And I'm burning, too. I lost him. And I lost my way.'

Suddenly, Eddie's eyelids were no longer glassy; he was awake and knew he had been dreaming. Yet his dream felt as if it had been more than a dream. It felt like a vision. Thin, straight lines of golden light shone through cracks in the boards on the other side of the glass. Outside, on the brown hillside, it was morning.

After breakfast the Carmodys wandered down the slope behind the house, up the opposite hillside and into the burned forest. Tara stalked on ahead, occasionally shouting over her shoulder.

'You could keep a horse here,' was one of the things she suddenly called. Years ago she had longed for a horse, but they had never had room for one.

'You know, it's beautiful – in its own way, that is,' said Mr Carmody, sounding puzzled by this observation.

Tara spun round, walking backwards in amazement.

'Beautiful?' she cried. 'Get real, Dad! Those Shocks burned their forest. And they didn't even make a good farm out of what was left.'

'It's certainly not great farming land,' agreed Mrs Carmody, who had lived on a farm herself when she was a child, but on a green, dairy farm, as easy to run as a farm could ever be.

'I don't think they tried very hard,' said Mr Carmody. 'They were always struggling. Independent, though! Toby was not only dead but buried before she ever let any of us know. She was . . . well . . . not hostile exactly, just aloof.'

'That's right! Blame the woman!' exclaimed Tara.

'No, it's nothing to do with blame,' said Mr Carmody. 'Everyone says she adored old Toby. But they kept to themselves . . . and to Shock Forest, of course.'

'What's that – that cage over there?' Eddie asked, pointing.

He was watching Tara who had come to a standstill beside a pen of some kind, fenced around with spiky iron railings.

'It's a – a grave,' said Mrs Carmody. She hesitated, then walked towards it.

'Guess whose?' asked Tara.

Inside the spikes of iron was a space about as big as a double bed. One grave was covered by a long, flat stone and the other by a mound of earth. Both graves were covered with leaves.

'Why didn't they just pack up and move to the city when they got older?' asked Mrs Carmody. 'It makes me sad, thinking of them struggling out here, looking at burned trees day after day.'

'They didn't look at them,' said Tara. 'The windows that overlook the forest are all boarded up.'

From the top of the long slope they could see sunburnt fingers of land stretching out, then folding in between one another. In the distance they could make out a slot of misty ocean.

'There's forest all the way to the sea,' said Eddie.

'Native bush,' Tara corrected him. 'Not high, though.'

'Gorse,' said their father. 'That's gorse and broom! People cleared the native trees, and the gorse and broom just cheered and took over. Mad colonists!'

'Why would anyone bring gorse to a new land?' Mrs Carmody asked. 'Well, let's be glad that we don't have that particular trouble on this hill.'

'Why don't we have gorse when everyone else does?' asked Eddie.

'Good question!' Mr Carmody looked from side to side, studying the different greens of the distant slopes, frowning. 'I suppose the Shocks must have sprayed it. Or grubbed it out.'

But thinking of the neglected hillside they had just climbed, it was hard to believe that Great Aunt Isobel Shock had cared whether gorse grew there or not.

'I thought I could hear the sea last night,' said Mrs Carmody at last, looking across to the sea, 'but now it looks too far away to be heard.'

'I heard it, too,' said Tara, 'but perhaps it was only the wind.'

'Yes . . . though nothing rattled,' Mrs Carmody pointed out. 'Things rattle in an old house.'

'Mysteries! Mysteries!' Mr Carmody sighed. 'No gorse! No rattling! Now listen – especially you, Tara! I know you're longing to get back to the city but I want to think things over, talk to a few people around here and find out just what possibilities there are.'

'I could feel this coming,' said Tara. 'Find someone who has a burnt-tree collection, and sell it. That's my advice.'

All the same she didn't sound as angry as she had yesterday. Eddie thought she sounded puzzled and even, if it were possible, a little scared.

Once again Eddie lay in bed, uncertain if his eyes were open or if he were looking through glass eyelids once more. Once again he was seeing that reddish flicker move restlessly over the walls and ceilings. And yet, if he turned his head sideways, there on the floor were his jeans and jacket, collapsed into a heap that still, somehow, had his own shape pressed into it . . . too real to be part of any dream. Perhaps it was not him but the air of his room that was dreaming – dreaming of fire.

Eddie corrected himself. Air could not dream. The white walls must be reflecting fire from somewhere else. Scrambling out of bed, he pressed his eye to the glass, lined it up with a crack and peered outside.

The hillside behind the house was burning. He could make out the shapes of great trees, their arms flung up in horror at what was happening to them. Their fingers burned, their skin burned, and now Eddie could hear once again that curious, soft roar that seemed to come, not merely from the other side of the glass, but from spaces inside the house as well – spaces that were *stealing* heat in order to set the ghostly fires roaring once more. That's why (even as he listened to the huge breath of the flames and shared the hillside's terrible, reviving memory) Eddie was shivering. Outside, burning trees lashed from side to side, as if in agony.

Eddie knew he must see all there was to see. He left the window, went downstairs, crossed the big room (dry leaves once more crackling under his feet) and went through the kitchen to the back door. It stood slightly open. Something moved on the other side of it, black against the trembling red.

A hand fell on his shoulder. Eddie thought he would die of fear. He turned with his cry still caught in his throat, and found himself staring into Tara's face.

She put a finger across her lips, as Eddie waved a shaking hand towards the door, then snatched up a broom from where it leaned against the kitchen bench and pushed the door open.

Great Uncle Toby Shock gazed back at them. He looked exactly like the young man in the photograph on the mantlepiece but he was burning like a tree – burning without actually being consumed, and giving off chill not warmth. His lips flickered as if they were made of flame, and when words came, they did so in the breathless, roaring voice of the fire. Their great-uncle was asking them a riddle.

'We went into the green and the green became red,
But inside the red I have hidden the green.
Give the green to the black where the green burned and bled.
What-will-be will grow out of time-that-has-been.'

Tara suddenly thrust the broom against the door, slamming it shut. The painted wood twitched and shivered as if it, too, could feel the cold.

The voice on the other side of the door sang a second riddle.

'Over the fire, there flies a bird,
And on the bird is a hook of horn,
And in the hook there lies a key.
Unlock the red and loose the green.'

And suddenly it was over. The door stopped quivering. The kitchen was filled with an ordinary darkness.

'Why does this ghost have to ask riddles?' asked Eddie, his voice shaking.

'We *hear* riddles,' Tara replied. 'It's because they don't match up with us. Anyhow, that second riddle's easy.'

Eddie followed her into the sitting room. Tara reached up and ran her fingers along the beak of the stuffed hawk. Something clinked as it tumbled away across the hearth and into the leaves on the carpet. She picked it up.

'A key!' she said. 'To unlock the red. But how can you unlock a fire?'

'I don't know,' said Eddie. He suddenly felt limp and heavy as if he must sleep. The riddles were working in him. He must sleep, and perhaps, in sleep, he might even dream the answers.

'Where do these leaves come from?' cried Mrs Carmody next morning. 'Leaves and ashes! Look at them!' She looked cross, but a little frightened, too. 'I swept this hearth yesterday, but it's messed up again.'

In the kitchen Eddie suddenly remembered the little hole he had seen watching him the first time he walked into the kitchen. Now he looked closely, he could see it was a keyhole in a door without a handle, flush with the wall and also painted red.

'I've found a door,' he called to Tara.

Tara had fastened the key to her charm bracelet. By holding her left hand close to the wall, and jiggling the key with her right, she unlocked the door.

'What have you found there?' asked Mrs Carmody. 'Oh, look! A spice cupboard! And spice jars!'

'Cloves and nutmegs!' said Tara. But she sounded doubtful. She pulled the cork from one of the jars. 'They're not green. They're all shrivelled up.'

'It says "kanuka" on this jar,' said Eddie, reading the labels. 'Kanuka, ngaio, cabbage tree . . .'

'Seeds,' said Mrs Carmody with sudden interest. 'Tree seeds. Get planting, kids. There's a big future in forestry.'

'It's not as funny as you might think,' said Mr Carmody. 'There is a future in forestry.'

'Those seeds are probably too old to grow,' Mrs Carmody said.

But Eddie was reaching for the spade behind the door. It seemed to leap into his hand.

'I'll plant them,' he offered. Tara watched him, frowning.

'I'll help,' she said. Eddie saw his father and mother look at her in amazement. But Tara didn't notice. She was thinking of something else. '*Out of the red*,' she muttered to Eddie, 'that red cupboard, for example, we'll *bring the green* . . . that's the seeds . . . and then we will see what there is to be seen. I read somewhere that seeds which have been buried in pyramids for three thousand years will still grow.'

Besides the spade, they found a small garden fork and a hoe propped against the wall just outside the back door. Together they began to dig on either side of the brick path that stretched out to the rusting clothes line. No one had dug there for a long time: the ground was hard and unwilling. Yet, finally, they finished digging it over, first with the spade, then with the fork, pulling out the long roots of twitch grass, smashing the lumps of soil with the back of the fork, and crumbling the smaller lumps with the hoe. As they worked, the seeds sat in a jar soaking in rainwater from the tank. That evening they planted them in two long, straight rows, one on either side of the path.

Later that night Eddie woke to hear, not a roar but a whisper, and the scratch of fingers at his window. Through last night's crack he saw the fire once more, but fainter and more distant. Something dark swayed backwards and forwards on the other side of the boards, but he couldn't make out what it was.

His door opened. Tara stood there, beckoning him to follow her downstairs and through the open kitchen door.

Trees again, but growing now, not burning. These trees reached forward to brush their faces with new bending twigs and young leaves. These trees welcomed them.

'Our seeds!' exclaimed Tara. 'These are our seeds. That's a cabbage tree, and I remember pushing cabbage-tree seeds into the dirt just there. I told them to grow, and they are growing. That's the tree my seed grew into.'

Together they stepped into a future forest. The air was softened with fine rain . . . nothing much more than a mist . . . smelling of wet leaves and soil and ferns. The trees went on and on and on.

'But we didn't plant all these,' Tara said, sounding puzzled.'

'We will, though,' Eddie cried, sure he was right. 'We'll plant more tomorrow. Shock Forest is starting all over again.'

Red light flowed towards them. They had come to a boundary between the green, growing forest of the future and the burning trees of the past. And there, on the boundary between growing and burning, sitting in her large, carved chair, was Great Aunt Isobel Shock. Time was her sitting room now. The stiff, springy hair that stood out around her face blazed angrily, yet Isobel Shock was shivering.

'I burned them!' she cried. Her teeth chattered, chopping the words short. 'They hate me. They hold me.'

'Who?' asked Eddie, amazed.

'The trees hate me,' she said. Tears, reflecting the flames, ran down her cheeks in smouldering lines.

'We were going to make a farm. We were going to live happily ever after. Why not? I know the Maori people said it was *tapu* and that no one should touch it, but land is meant to be used. And then – and then the forest *bewitched* Toby. He'd walk among the trees, and come back happy. *I* wouldn't walk with him. Why should I learn to love the trees? That land they were growing on was meant to be our farm. But, at last, one dry, summer day when Toby was in town and the wind was blowing towards the sea, I did go into the forest . . . went into the forest carrying paper and petrol and matches. The trees whispered to me, but I wouldn't listen. Not me! I crumpled the paper . . . piled the sticks . . . poured the petrol. "Tssst!" went the match. The forest burned and burned and burned. It turned to ashes. Toby drove up, and, as we stood side by side watching it burn, I felt something inside Toby turning to ashes, too.'

She fell silent.

'What happened after that?' asked Eddie.

'After that?' said Great Aunt Isobel. 'Nothing happened except that we grew older. The forest is still burning. Our farm never thrived. Toby died.'

Her voice was growing fainter.

'I can hear his voice calling my name, but the forest is holding me.'

Then, suddenly, she began to burn all over, twitching and twisting in the embrace of the fire.

Tara caught Eddie's arm and they ran down the hill, under their cool trees, and back to the house again.

At breakfast, Mr Carmody said he was going to talk to the man at the shop.

'I'll come, too,' said Tara. 'I'll open the gate.'

'Now, *there's* a change,' said Mr Carmody. Tara grinned.

'I've had gate-opening experience,' she said. 'You might wreck the delicate hinges.'

Eddie and his mother put more seeds to soak in a jam jar, then walked on the sunny hillside among the blackened tree trunks.

'How would you feel about staying on here?' his mother asked cautiously. 'Dad's wondering about using his redundancy money to set up a tree nursery of some kind.'

'I wouldn't mind,' said Eddie.

As they wandered back again, feeling unexpectedly as if they were coming home, Mr Carmody and Tara came home, too. It was a long time since Eddie had seen his father so cheerful and excited.

'Colin says there's going to be a big demand for young trees in a year or two,' he declared 'He says . . .'

'Hang on a moment!' said Mrs Carmody. 'Who's Colin?'

'The man at the shop,' explained Mr Carmody. 'He says there'll be a big demand for hardwoods. He's got a stand of hardwoods himself. They take longer to grow than *pinus* but it would be a retirement fund for us. And in the meantime we could work up a few market lines. We'd need a shade house. And we'd need more water, but Colin says we'd probably find ground water if we sink a drill.'

'They've got *horses*,' cried Tara. 'Jake and Lisa, I mean. Lisa's horse is a chestnut mare called Zipper . . .'

'Who are Jake and Lisa?' asked Eddie.

'They live at the shop,' said Tara. 'Lisa's just the same age as me . . . Jake's a bit older.' She caught Eddie's eye for a moment, then looked away.

That night Eddie woke to hear a whisper at his window, and knew it was the sound of trees murmuring to one another. He went to the window and, half experimentally, tried to push it open. To his surprise it actually moved a little. He gave it one slow, steady, strong push, and it burst open. The boards that had closed it in for so long fell outwards; they had quite rotted through.

Eddie looked on to a hillside covered with trees. They swung towards him like a dark wave surging forwards though without actually moving. The sound of the wind in their branches was like the sound of the sea.

Eddie breathed in. He felt as if he were breathing pure happiness. It filled his lungs, swept up into his head and overflowed outwards to his very fingertips.

'*I* planted you,' he cried to the trees, and they seemed to recognize his voice and bend a little towards him, letting him know that they realized who he was.

Something moved below him. Eddie looked down.

An old man and old woman, walking arm in arm, came out of the forest. He watched them as they moved towards the house, and wondered if he should go down and open the door for them. As he hesitated, they looked up at his window and waved and smiled before they looked at each other once more. They did not hesitate but kept on walking away from the forest, growing more and more transparent with every step they took, until they finally dissolved into the night air.

Eddie stared, knowing he would never again see Shock Forest quite like this except in his dreams, for the lives of men are short and the lives of trees are long.

'Never mind! You're on your way,' he told the forest at last. 'And you've got a new name. People will call you Carmody Bush.'

And then he went to bed and slept peacefully in the warm wind that blew through his open window . . . slept without dreaming, while outside the kitchen door, the patient seeds drank and swelled and began their long climb towards the sun.

Long Wing

Elizabeth Laird

Illustrated by Alan Lee

THE HUGE wave crashed against the jagged black rocks and a plume of spray rose high into the air. A sudden sharp squall picked it up and hurled its tiny droplets of water and salt on to the tough tussocky grass that grew on the slopes high above.

Sky King, sitting on his rough nest of twigs and moss, had been half asleep, but the spray woke him and turning his head he scanned the long grey expanse of sea. His mate had been gone for more than a week and hunger was making him uneasy.

He shifted his body, but he had moved too quickly and the precious egg, that for days past had been slowly splitting open under the weak assaults from the chick struggling inside, threatened to roll out of the nest. Gently, Sky King prodded it back into place, settled himself again and resumed his long wait.

And then he felt a feeble fluttering, as something moved under him. The chick, his chick, was hatching. Carefully, he stepped aside. The baby albatross's hooked bill had finally cut a long breach in the confining case of shell and the stubby rudiments of two wings, covered in wet down, were free at last. Weak from the effort, dazzled by the light and smells and sounds of the world, the baby staggered out from his shell and took his first stumbling step.

Sky King had been so intent on the birth of his son that he had not seen Silver, his mate, approach, but she was suddenly beside him, bending her great white neck, nuzzling the baby with her long hooked bill. Gently she forced up his head. The chick opened his beak and she squirted a stream of rich warm oil from her stomach into his.

Sky King could wait no longer. He had to get back to sea and feed before hunger made him weak. He waddled on his great grey webbed feet, speckled with unusual stains of brown, to the top of the grassy slope and spread out his huge wings. He began to run downhill and the wind caught him and lifted him into flight. He circled the headland once, looking down on his mate and his newly hatched son, then he turned away and soared off into the great Southern Ocean.

The autumn and winter had passed for Long Wing in endless days of waiting for his parents to come winging home to the nest with food for his ravenous stomach.

At first, either Sky King or Silver had stayed with him all the time, sheltering him under their soft warm breasts from the fierce spring blizzards that sometimes whipped across the headland, and seeing off with furious squawks and flappings of their giant wings the rapacious skuas, who came with sharp beaks and vicious claws to tear and devour any unprotected chicks. But as the months had passed and Long Wing had grown, his parents, needing to find ever greater quantities of food for his huge appetite, had left him for longer and longer intervals.

The winter had been long and terrible. Far to the south, ice had spread out in great white sheets across the freezing sea. Stinging flakes of snow had swept continuously over the bare headland, driven on violent winds from the chill Antarctic wastes. Alone on his nest, a giant ball of fluffy white down, Long Wing had sat and waited to be fed, hunkered down in his fluff through the long nights, spending the short days gazing out to sea, watching for his father or mother's return.

In that time, he had moved through many transformations, growing first into a vast ball of downy fluff, then slowly putting forth feathers and long slim wings, developing a powerful beak on which ribbed nostrils lay like delicate flutes along each side.

It had been many days now since his parents had visited him. Silver had flown away weeks earlier, and since then Long Wing had seen Sky King only once. He had landed reluctantly, his gorge only half full, and had needed much persuasion, much tapping on the bill and many shrill cries, before he would regurgitate it for his rapacious chick.

Long Wing was hungry, and another sensation, a kind of curiosity, was growing inside him too. He watched, head tilted on one side, as another albatross from a nearby nest site ran expertly down the slope, its wings outstretched, and soared away into the wind.

He had been batting his wings for weeks in practice, and he was beginning to trust in their strength. Raising them experimentally, and hesitating frequently to look about him, Long Wing waddled slowly to the edge of the cliff. He stood there for a long time as if screwing up his courage, then he held his untried wings invitingly up to the wind. A squall caught him. He was lifted off his feet for a moment, but the wind suddenly dropped again. He would have plunged helplessly down the sheer cliff to his death on the sharp mussel-covered rocks below if a last little gust had not caught him and blown him back on to the grass.

He had not felt any fear. The short sensation of being airborne had been good. The lull had only lasted a moment or two. He could feel the wind again now, ruffling his feathers, and it excited him. More boldly, he spread his wings out again and took a couple of lolloping strides towards the edge of the cliff. This time the wind picked him up securely in its friendly grasp and he felt for the first time its rushing power as he let it carry him up and away.

He tried to copy the older birds as they circled round the headland, using their motionless wings as sails, picking up every nuance of the turbulent flow of air, but he was too clumsy, too untried. He found himself swooping down, closer and closer to the sea.

He had not realized, from his eyrie up on the cliff, that the sea moved so strangely, that the cold green landscape rocked up and down, making the waves of the air above it, on which his wings were relying, falter and ripple in such unfamiliar, unpredictable ways. He was so low now that one webbed foot dipped into the sea. He flapped his wings twice, trying to pull himself up, but the air currents were against him and he gave in to the inevitable and sank down on to the water.

It was a new sensation, floating on the shifting transparent surface, his feet piercing through it as he learned to ride the waves. He sat on the water and looked about, getting used to the moving walls of grey green swell, the patterns of white foam on their gleaming sides and the endlessly changing horizon.

Then something caught his eye. A pale shape, round at one end with short streamer-like projections at the other, flickered through the water, almost under his bill. He plunged at it curiously, and the hooked end of his bill touched it. The thing jerked away and shimmered down into the dark depths. But Long Wing had caught a taste of it. It was a squid, his favourite food, the thing his parents had so often dropped down his gulping throat. Excited, and urgent with hunger, he paddled himself forwards, his eyes on the water, looking for another.

He was surprised by a sudden noise behind him. A shag shot out of the water at speed, running on tiptoe across the waves to take off, shrieking a piercing cry of danger. Though it made Long Wing uneasy, he did not understand where the danger might come from and he stayed sitting, confused, not seeing the long fin that was speeding towards him, breaking through the surface of the wave.

The shark rose up under him, jaws agape, and it would have caught him if a lucky buffet from the choppy wind had not suddenly knocked him out of range of the rows of sharp teeth. Terrified, Long Wing twisted and turned, struggling to take off, but he had no idea how to lift himself up into the air. The shark whipped round and was on him again. Long Wing was in its mouth now. Its jaws were closing on his body.

Long Wing twisted his neck frantically from side to side. The only moving thing in the smooth grey surface of the shark's head was its small round eye. Desperately, he jabbed at it with the full force of his bill. The shark's grip faltered. It dived, trying to take Long Wing with it, to drown him in the depths where it could eat him in peace, but Long Wing pecked furiously again at the rolling eye.

The shark, moving more slowly this time, made one last effort, wheeling round in the water to come up behind Long Wing, but the young albatross's every sense was now alive with terror and rage and he turned and raised his huge wings, lowering his bill, ready for the fight.

The shark had had enough. It sped away through the water, its fin hidden almost at once by a wave. Long Wing had had enough too. He held his wings up to the wind, as if he was begging it to lift him into the friendlier sky, but he was in a trough now between two waves and the air was still. He raised himself out of the water and began to paddle, then run, frantically over the surface, wings outstretched. The water trough beneath him was rising now into the crest of the next wave and as it rose to the top a gust of wind picked him up and carried him into its welcoming currents.

The summer was good to Long Wing. Soaring alone on huge outstretched wings round the great southern oceans of the world, travelling sometimes hundreds of miles in a single day, he learned to know every trick of the wind, to use every gust, every flutter of turbulence. In the violent storms that turned the sea into shifting mountain ranges of water, he would swoop down the long trough between two waves, eyes alert for the pale flash of a dead squid floating on the surface, or a rolling swarm of prawn-like krill. He would follow whales, ready to snap up any titbits that floated out of their vast jaws, flying low over icebergs that lumbered through the sea like huge sculptures, shot through with blue and green light, their walls scoured and carved by the salt waves that smacked endlessly against their frozen sides.

Sometimes he saw other birds of his kind. He joined them occasionally as they squabbled round the offal flung from the deck of a fishing boat, and once, circling round a trawler, waiting for the magical supply of food to appear, he met his father.

They had landed together on the water and thrust out their necks, their bills wide open, calling to each other with loud croaking cries. And then the food had showered down on them from the deck above and they had joined the other snapping, voracious birds at the feast.

He never saw his mother.

More than two years had passed since Long Wing had flown the nest. He had survived his third winter at sea and was ready for another spring. He was a powerful bird now, still immature but experienced, a skilful fisher, a brilliant navigator of the wind.

While Long Wing soared aloft, his eyes ever scanning the water for signs of food, ten thousand miles to the north two men were working on the covered deck of a big ship. They were too used to the stench of fish that had penetrated every corner of the vessel to be properly nauseated but they turned their faces into the breeze whenever they had the chance to breathe gusts of cleaner air.

'You've signed up for the whole season?'

The man with the mole on his cheek straightened his back and stood up. His companion, still bending over the oily mechanism on the ship's vast empty deck, looked up at him.

'Sure. You mean you haven't?'

Mole Cheek shrugged, watching with interest as the other man deftly manoeuvred the mechanism's complex parts with his eight remaining fingers.

'Yeah,' he said. 'I've signed. The money's good.'

'You're not married, then?'

Mole Cheek screwed a roll of saliva up on his tongue and spat it out over the side of the ship.

'What if I am? She gets the money. Some of it. What else does she want?'

Eight Fingers said nothing. He turned the last nut with his spanner and stood up. Mole Cheek watched curiously as he wiped his oily fingers on a cloth.

'How did you lose them, anyway?'

'What? These?' Eight Fingers held up his right hand. The first and second fingers had been sliced off at the lowest joint. Only a couple of short stumps remained. 'Caught them in the winch last season. Bringing in a catch of tuna. Biggest I ever saw and I've seen some. Took my eye off what I was doing for a couple of seconds and a hook whipped round . . .'

'OK.' Mole Cheek had looked away. 'I get the picture.'

'Funny thing was,' Eight Fingers said, 'it was all the fault of a damned bird. We were bringing the line in, full of tuna, and there was this dead bird, a silver-coloured thing, caught on one of the hooks. Another one, a great feathered monster with speckled brown stains on its feet, flew right down to it. It kept pecking at the man who was getting the dead one off the hook. The others tried to beat it off but it wouldn't go. I was so busy laughing at them all, slipping around in all the tuna blood, slapping away at this crazy bird that I took my eyes off the job and the next thing I knew . . .'

'Yeah,' said Mole Cheek quickly. 'What kind of bird did you say it was?'

'Albatross. It was weird, you know . . .'

'What? What was weird?'

Eight Fingers put down his rag and began to walk across the clanging metal deck towards the companionway.

'It was almost as if the thing was – oh, I don't know – demented. With rage or grief or something.'

'Maybe the dead one was its mate or something.'

'Its mate? Don't be soft. It was a bird, not some bloody Romeo.'

As the fleets of trawlers from the fish-hungry nations of the north began their long journey all the way down the world towards the tuna killing fields of the Southern Ocean, the days started to lengthen into the coming spring.

Long Wing was restless. All through the dark months of winter he had flown and hunted alone, meeting other birds only when he raced them to snatch the best morsels that fell from the occasional trawler into the sea. But now he was aware of his own kind as never before.

On a day when a sharp spring breeze was blowing and the sunlight splintered on the rippling water (calmer now than it had been for months) he watched as a young female flew below him, her black tipped wings dazzling white against the blue sea.

He dropped down to her altitude and followed her. She was circling round a group of six or eight other albatrosses who were bobbing about on the surface of the sea close together, gesticulating excitedly, although there was no shoal of fish that Long Wing could see, no floating carcass to be dismembered, no boiling mass of krill.

The female ahead wheeled round and swooped down to land beside them. At once a young male bird paddled enthusiastically up to her. He stretched his head up as high as it would go, waggling it excitedly from side to side. She turned away, and he raised himself out of the water and stretched out his wings, curving them towards her and calling loudly.

Long Wing, wanting for the first time the company of other birds, but too young to understand their excitement, dropped down on to the water beside the young female. He stretched his head and called as he had seen the older birds do, and lifted his wings and beat them once or twice. But the others, seeing the dark brown tips to his feathers and knowing he was only a juvenile who would not breed for years yet, ignored him and went on with their dancing display.

Long Wing stayed among the party of albatrosses all through the spring day, excited and content. They took off as evening came, some singly, some in pairs, leaving him alone on the water.

As luck would have it, a passing pair of sperm whale, who had gorged themselves on squid earlier that day, released dozens of them from their gaping mouths. The lifeless squid floated to the surface and Long Wing feasted that night as he had never done before.

The men had worked all day on the covered deck of the fishing vessel, spearing bait on to thousands of hooks. The baited lines lay in holding trays along the deck, ready to be paid out into the ocean. The men were hungry and thirsty. Their backs ached and their fingers were numb with cold. Above all, their tempers were foul.

'Frozen!' said Eight Fingers in disgust, tipping a box full of rock-hard fish on to the deck.

'So what if it is?' growled Mole Cheek, picking up a piece of stiff flesh and ramming it on to a razor-sharp hook.

'So it won't sink, that's what,' spat Eight Fingers, 'so the bloody birds'll plunge for it, so we'll pull in a line of dead albatrosses tomorrow instead of tuna, so bang goes our bonus. That's what.'

Mole Cheek looked briefly at the narrow strip of sea and sky that was visible through the long opening in the stern of the covered deck. A flock of albatrosses flew low over the water, waiting for bounty to fall from the ship.

'And there they are, the stupid gits, lining up to get it.'

'My heart bleeds,' said Eight Fingers, holding up his mutilated hand. 'They owe me for this. Give me a gun and I'd shoot the lot of them.'

When darkness fell the lines began to pay out as the ship moved slowly ahead through the water, leaving the murderous snaking trail, eighty mile long, in its wake.

By dawn the first part of the line of baited hooks had sunk down into the sea and from some of them huge, heavy tuna fish already hung, twitching in their death throes. But the fish on the last part of the line, nearest to the ship, were still partially frozen. They floated near the surface, deadly snares, and as the sky lightened, the flock of twenty or thirty albatrosses and shearwaters, who had spent the night close to the ship waiting for the food to appear, caught sight of them and began to plunge down towards the baited hooks that were still just a few feet below the surface of the water.

Long Wing had been flying all night, half sleeping on the wing, and it was well after dawn when he saw, far below, the big ship, chugging gently through the water. He made for it like an arrow, plunging down through the turbulent air to the place where a few birds were still squawking near the stern.

Only half the original flock were left. The others, the strongest ones, who had been able to fight off the smaller, weaker birds in the scramble for the bait, had already drowned, their bills caught in the deadly hooks.

But now the last section of line was sinking fast, pulled under by the weight of dead tuna and dead birds. Long Wing could see, disappearing tantalizingly out of sight, a morsel of fish that tempted him. He lowered his head, ready to dive for it, but he was too late. A shearwater, flying low over head, had seen it too. It folded its wings and plunged like an arrow in front of Long Wing's eyes, caught the fish in its mouth, struggled desperately for a moment or two as the hook bit deep into its throat, and died.

Long Wing took off into the wind. He circled a few times round the ship but the line had sunk now and there was no other sign that food would be forthcoming. Disappointed, he wheeled away and headed east, flying low over the water. Yesterday, 300 miles away to the east, he had found a rich source of krill. He would go back that way today and try his luck again.

Ten years had passed since Long Wing had first struggled out of his egg. His dark brown juvenile plumage had long since given way to the brilliant white feathers of adulthood and his powerful bill was now a formidable fishing weapon. His magnificent black-tipped wings, that spanned three metres at full stretch, had mastered every subtle alteration of wind and air and his tireless strength could carry him for thousands of miles on endless soaring flights around the great southern oceans of the world.

But Long Wing was not flying now. He had come in to land. Like a pigeon returning to its loft, he had flown home to the cliff top where he had fledged.

He had been at sea for so long that his first landing on the grassy headland had been clumsy, and he might have crushed a leg if a lucky hummock of tussocky grass had not broken his fall.

He had chosen his nest site immediately. It had not been hard to find, a good grassy spot, sheltered from the wind. He had had to drive away another questing male, but he had done this without much difficulty, and his first effort at building had gone well. There were useful ferns and twigs and tussock grass lying all around.

It took Long Wing days to make his nest and it was far from finished when the first female arrived. Her mate, an older male on a nest site not far from Long Wing's, put up his wings and raucously called her in. She flew down beside him and they greeted each other with an ecstatic display of cries and gestures before they mated.

Long Wing watched the sky constantly, waiting for Wind Hover to appear. He had met her two years ago, when with other juveniles he had returned to the headland to be with his kind, and he had courted her all through the long kindly days of last summer. They had circled each other in slow dances, had whistled and called and tapped their beaks. They had flown together, diving and soaring, wheeling and plunging in perfect unison, as if they were two parts of the same creature. And then the autumn storms had driven them apart, to fish and fly alone through the long Antarctic winter.

All along the rocky headland, albatross pairs were busy, repairing nests, greeting each other, dancing out the rituals that bonded them together. Long Wing walked restlessly round and round his nest, his eyes on the sky.

And then he saw her. She came in below the clouds, flying on the wind, her black eyes searching the crowded headland, looking for him. Long Wing lifted his head and called. For a moment Wind Hover seemed not to hear him and he called again, louder and more urgently. She wheeled round, looking for a place to land, and came down at last beside him.

For a moment or two they cried out loudly to each other, their heads raised, then Long Wing tugged gently at Wind Hover's wing feathers and she turned to face him, her bill slightly open, and they ducked and rolled their heads, softly touching each other. Wind Hover lifted her head to the sky, inviting Long Wing to groom her, and he dropped his bill into the soft mottled feathers on her neck, nibbling and stroking, perfectly content.

Later that day, they mated.

The large blotched egg had become the centre of Long Wing's life. Since Wind Hover had laid it, eleven weeks earlier, he had hardly seen her. As soon as she had come back to the nest from days of feeding out at sea, he had been driven by his own hunger to go in search of food.

She had never been gone for more than four days before, and he had seldom left her for more than three, though he had sometimes had to travel five hundred miles in that time in search of a proper feed.

But this time it was different. Wind Hover had been gone for nearly two weeks. Fretting with anxiety, Long Wing scanned the sky, calling to her from time to time, though he could see she was not there. He could not wait much longer. He had to feed soon.

Gingerly, he lifted himself up off his egg. For some days past, he had been aware that something was happening inside the thick shell. He had been excited by faint sounds of tappings and scratchings.

His movement seemed to rouse the unhatched chick and Long Wing heard a series of clicks and taps as its soft bill resumed the exhausting work of breaking through the shell. Gently, he laid his own bill against it, feeling the vibration of the struggling movements within.

He hesitated and looked up again into the sky. Where was Wind Hover? When would she come? He lowered himself again on to his egg, protecting it with his great body from the keen spring wind that ripped across the headland, but a moment later he was up again. His hunger was desperate now. He had to feed before he became too weak to fly.

He stepped awkwardly off his nest and fumbled at the egg with his beak. Every instinct was urging him to stay with it. Every pang of hunger was ordering him to go.

He lifted his head and gave one long despairing cry, calling for Wind Hover, pleading for his chick, then, without a backward glance, he spread out his wings, ran down into the wind and soared away out to sea.

A thousand miles away, the rusting hulk of a fishing boat was steaming through the water, winching on board an endless line of twitching tuna fish.

'One for you!' Mole Cheek called out, unhooking a dead albatross and throwing its bedraggled body to the man beside him.

'Leave off, will you?' growled Eight Fingers, and picking up Wind Hover's body, he flung it out over the stern of the ship where it sank down into the sea.

A Singer from the Desert Came

Jamila Gavin

Illustrated by Peter Sis

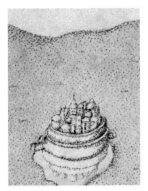

'I MET an Angel the other day.' The traveller looked around, pausing to see what effect his words had on the assembled company. They surrounded him eagerly, their faces hollowed out by the flickering firelight. Their eyes, like dark mirrors stitched into their pale plastic-coated skins, reflected him over and over.

People didn't talk about angels these days – nor about God. They only wanted to talk about their fears. Whenever travellers happened by their city, they wanted to know how it fared in the Desert World. Were their any signs of regeneration? Was anything growing? How long were other groups surviving? That's what they had come to hear – outside the city walls, in the no-man's-land where strangers were allowed to camp for awhile. He knew that before the evening was over, they would ask the dreaded question.

But his statement seemed to wrap them into a thoughtful silence – as if they had forgotten what an angel was; and each one was ruminating over the word, trying to recall what it meant. So the traveller took up his stringed instrument and began to sing.

'I met an angel the other day.
He was made of
Water and blood and bone,
And skin and sinew and muscle
And iron and tin and zinc
And air and earth and fire
And liquid gold.

And when he sang, his voice
Like pinprick stars
Pierced the heaven of my heart.
And when he sang, notes
Hollow and dark
From subterranean depths
Shuddered when he sang.

I met an angel the other day
Whose feet were on the ground.
I was flying
I was flying
I was flying.'

The voice of the troubadour rose upwards, like the words of his song, and broke into falsetto, making the back of the neck prickle as it soared like a hunting bird. Suddenly he was down in the depths, gravelly low, as if the notes were formed in the hollows of his stomach. His long fingers plucked and fingered the thin strings. Then his voice died away and he let the sounds of his instrument wander on awhile, resonating, before expiring into a soft last chord.

Silence; a held breath; then a gasp, and a sob broke from somewhere. His voice had that magic; that ability to touch and reach into people's souls. His song reminded them of Orph.

At last, someone asked the inevitable question. 'Never mind angels, did you come across any . . .?'

Above the outline of the canyons, where a desert sky stretched like silk from one horizon to another, they saw 'Perdita' passing in orbit as it had done every evening for the past sixty years, barely distinguishable from the evening star which glimmered in the darkening sky.

'They're coming nearer,' said Martin, our father. He tried to sound unemotional. 'The troubadour saw them in the valley beyond the canyon. If they were determined enough, they could be here by midday tomorrow.' His words hung in the air, their meaning filtering through to our brains and our stomachs.

I looked at our mother, Lara. Her face was ashen and she pressed her hands across her abdomen as if in pain. Then she rushed from the room and I heard her retching outside.

'They' were the Arifi people. That was the effect they had on us. All our lives, we had known this would happen. But somehow unpleasant knowledge can be set aside. We had all found it easier to be complacent and not think that one day we would be the victims of our own folly. It was the way we lived in our own little oasis of civilization; enclosed in our own green enclave of safe, unpolluted, fertile land; living in a false sense of security within our city state. It's not that we didn't have the knowledge, we did – but chose not to think about it. We knew what lay outside beyond the canyons and across the rolling sand dunes of the desert. We knew about the other tribes of people starving, dying of radiation and disease, struggling to survive; who would, if they could, seek refuge in our safe enclave. But we ruthlessly kept them out. Some of us argued that we should be prepared to share our wealth and our knowledge, but others insisted there simply wasn't enough to go round. The others won the argument. So we had become a small fortress state; turning in on ourselves; spying on ourselves; watching and listening, not just in public places, but in our homes and work places too, as if we had an enemy within as well as without. We nursed an obsessive fear of outsiders – especially the people of the Arifi.

We called them the Arifi because they lived in the desert – which most of the world had now become; because their skins had yellowed and dried with disease, and ultraviolet rays, and lack of vitamins; because when they advanced across the sandy landscape, they moved like the Arifi dust storms from North Africa, in a great whirling, impenetrable cloud, sucking up and swallowing anything in its path. The Arifi people were not builders, they were destroyers. They had no faith in a future, but lived for the day. They were the dispossessed from a once industrial world, reduced now to being marauding nomads who robbed and stripped the earth. They moved like marcher ants, consuming everything and leaving nothing behind them.

This is what we had been brought up to believe. I didn't know anyone who had seen an Arifi and sometimes I was curious; sometimes I wondered about them.

Although the aim of our founders had been to keep our location a secret, it was inevitable that one day the Arifi would hear about us and track us down, for there were always the travellers – little troupes of people, often just extended families, who preferred to fend for themselves rather than link up with a larger group or tribe. They would turn up from time to time, like this troubadour. Then we would allow them their legislated twenty-one days of hospitality outside the city walls, and send them on their way again. We knew this meant word would get out one day.

The assembly had once discussed putting travellers to death to protect our secret state. But I'm glad to say this was defeated. However, we did escort them out into the wilderness and leave them without the means to know from which direction they had come and where they could safely go. So many must have perished anyway. But there was always the risk that some got through to tell of our existence.

So now we live in dread.

A year ago came the first positive sighting. A small group of travellers seeking refuge under our twenty-one day rule, told us about seeing a long column of Arifi people crossing the salt marshes – driven in desperation from a desert land which even they could no longer survive in. The travellers had managed to evade them by hiding in caves.

Months went by and we had no further visitations or sightings until the arrival of the solitary troubadour with his appalling news.

When Lara re-appeared she had regained control of herself. She had washed and put on a white home-spun cotton dress – almost as if she had prepared herself for sacrifice. She came and stood next to our father, Martin.

Lara and Martin were not our real parents. Hardly anyone over the age of thirteen had parents who were still alive; so new parents were allocated. Often they were barely more than fifteen or sixteen themselves. We were a society of children. Only Orph had lived to what used to be called an old age. He was eighty when he died – can you believe it? *Eighty!* No one lived that long now. Twenty was average, thirty if you were lucky. Something got you – usually some kind of cancer. I've already got skin cancer, despite my plastic coating. We all get it sooner or later. And if cancer doesn't get you, asthma does or brain disease, or our immune system collapses.

'Navarth has called a meeting at the Assembly Hall,' Martin told us.

'Everyone over the age of eight can attend.'

'Oh good!' cried my little brother Rhett. 'That means I can go.'

I shrugged with annoyance. Normally only people over the age of twelve attended, but it showed how serious things were if they had brought down the age. I was thirteen, and hadn't yet attended my first assembly, so I couldn't help feeling a bit miffed.

Martin made me change into a white linen tunic like Lara, though Rhett stayed as he was in green.

'Why?' I asked. 'Are we going to die?' I thought we only wore white tunics for death.

'It's just ceremonial,' said Martin, then he and Lara wouldn't answer any more questions. They just urged us to hurry and held each other's hands as if for support.

All four of us joined a throng of citizens making their way to the Assembly Hall. Many wore white tunics. I wanted to ask lots of questions but no one was talking. All I could hear was the footfall of hundreds of people. The silence frightened me.

We reached the Assembly Hall. It was a strange circular structure created out of a multiplicity of recycled and regurgitated materials: paper, wood, metal, wool, glass, stone and alabaster – all moulded and pressed and shaped and carved and sculpted. It looked as flimsy as cobweb, yet somehow indestructible. I had seen it from the outside many times, and had always thought that it was like a gigantic wasp's nest or some strange fossilized brain.

On entering, we found ourselves in a vast complex structure of chambers and passages, dark and sticky like resin, as if we walked through the labyrinth of a mind.

Suddenly we were plunged into a daylight brightness. I was blinded for a moment. It was the main chamber. Slowly I opened my eyes. I was overawed: its size, its beauty, circular, vast. There was space for every citizen to sit, on tiers of steps which rippled upwards towards the glass domed roof.

In the centre sat Navarth, on a great carved gold chair – The Oracle Chair. I had heard of it. It must have been right there that Orph had sung – and by his singing, exerted such power that he controlled everyone's hearts and minds. I had tried many times to imagine what his voice sounded like. Why, oh why, did he die before I could hear him!

Navarth looked alone and sad. We all depend on her now that Orph is dead. She is only sixteen, but you never know who will emerge as leader. Orph, when he was alive, had always recommended Navarth. He told the Council that Navarth was their natural leader after him. She had been his assistant, and he had imparted all his knowledge to her. But by this time, Orph was so ancient that our increasingly youthful society thought he was too old and out of touch to know best. When he died they ignored his advice and chose Alder. We all paid the price. Alder was nineteen, rash and stupid – though some thought he was brave and heroic. He was always wanting a fight. It was he who generated terror inside us – especially of the Arifi. He kept it fanned, as though he gained power through other's anxieties. Not so long ago, his fear-mongering led us into a futile conflict with a group of travellers who had made a determined attempt to settle within our twenty-five mile exclusion zone. Our enemy was ill, starving and desperate, and prepared to die in their effort to overrun us if we wouldn't share our wealth.

Navarth would have found an option. She would have negotiated; given them some knowledge and technical help. But Alder believed such tactics only encouraged them to come back for more. 'A clear message must be sent out to them and anyone else – to stay away. Otherwise,' he declared, 'it will be the Arifi next – and then what?'

His strategy nearly had us wiped out. Overwhelmed by their numbers, Alder resorted to the use of chemical-weapons. Because of him, a whole swathe of fertile land was devastated and Alder himself was killed. A lot of our people and theirs too died; horribly.

Seeing how we almost faced extinction once more, our assembly representatives finally turned to Navarth to take the Oracle's Chair.

But was it too late?

I looked at her with awe. It wasn't so long ago that she had helped to teach me in the school. That's how our school system worked. It was the 'Orph system'. He taught us to be both teachers and pupils for ever.

But today something was wrong – very, very wrong. There was a death-like solemnity, such as I had only witnessed when Orph died. I felt a frisson of barely concealed panic shudder through everyone. I had never experienced such a sense of terror.

I began to hear the word 'Arifi' whispered fearfully. Just the sound made me shiver as it hissed in my ears like a fiery desert wind. People didn't know whether to stay put or gather together family and belongings and flee into the hills.

A debate began – fitfully – barely under control. Navarth struggled for calm and sanity during the discussion.

Speaker after speaker gave their opinions. Some wrung their hands in defeat. Others yelled accusations of cowardice. Emotions overflowed. Voices ranted with anger.

'Face the enemy, fight.'

'We have our technology. It has protected us so far.'

'Yes, but then, we were just keeping a few hundred at bay. Now it's millions,' others argued.

'Our technology is useless against such numbers,' agreed the technocrats.

'We should have killed all travellers as Alder would have done!' a voice declared. 'We shouldn't have listened to those goody-goody liberals with their humanist ideas. Look where it's got us!' There was a roar of agreement.

'There's one of them out there now. That troubadour. How do we know he's not a spy?'

There was a moan of support and people looked at each other as if to reinforce their anxiety.

'We still have our nuclear weapon,' a citizen reminded the forum.

All eyes turned to the Ark which had a permanent place on the round table.

'Are you mad?' Navarth reeled with shock. 'What do you think this is all about? How do you think we got to this state in the first place?'

It was two nuclear accidents in quick succession, one in Russia and one in France which had returned nearly all of us back to the Stone Age in my great-great-grandfather's time.

My little brother Rhett asked 'Why?' He was too young to have reached that stage in his history lessons. 'Why can't we just nuke them?'

'Because, dear little brother, it would kill us too,' I hissed in his ear.

'We should have made a deal with them up there!' another citizen prodded the air above his head.

Every face in the assembly tilted up and gazed open-mouthed through the glass dome to the evening sky beyond. In a few minutes, 'Perdita' would rise, just a little ahead of the moon and would glow as a constant reminder of the safety of a privileged few.

Just days before the Great Devastation, a group of technocrats, politicians and wealthy business tycoons, had vacated the planet. They had known for at least nine decades that this would happen, and had secretly planned their escape. The so-called Space Programme which began in the 1950s and '60s, was all part of a plan to build a huge artificial planet which could sustain up to a hundred thousand specially picked people. It was never space exploration for its own sake. It was always a plan which anticipated the end of the world. As the millennium drew to a close, what with pollution and ozone depletion, it became clear that there would be some kind of catastrophe – human or natural which could happen at any time and destroy all life.

So a secret agenda had been drawn up to prepare 'Perdita', the man-made planet. It would be launched into space and left orbiting the sun until it was required as a safe haven for those who could negotiate or buy themselves a place on it.

By the end, the experts knew to the very day when the catastrophe would come. A number of shuttle space craft bearing the chosen few secretly took off from several corners of the earth, and all rendezvoused in space with Perdita. Thirty years later, Perdita made contact with us. Despite all their fancy technology, their population was falling and they were looking to set a quota for taking on more people. They had watched our progress from space and now wanted us to join forces. They suggested a fixed number be allocated every decade and shuttled to Perdita.

Orph had rejected them contemptuously. He refused to have anything to do with those who had gone there. He felt that the powerful and wealthy had put all those skills and resources into saving their own skins, instead of ensuring the safety of Earth. He said, better to be annihilated than perpetuate such an abomination. It's the only time Orph was known to act less than democratically. He simply told the forum, 'I shall leave this place for the desert if you insist on making such a deal.'

I know now that there were already those who whispered, 'We can wait. He'll soon be going anyway. He can't live for ever.' As I sat here in awe and wonderment on my first visit to Orph's own Assembly Hall, I could hardly believe what I heard. Voices cried out unashamedly.

'We should have been developing our own technology to leave this planet.'

'Orph deluded us with his ancient knowledge. We should have known that the past had nothing more to teach us.'

There was a stunned silence. Orph had never been criticized like this before.

You see, Orph was a legend – like Moses. His name was synonymous with Law, Scholarship and Purpose. He brought us all up to believe that we must somehow pass on some semblance of what human beings could be – the best of them, not the worst.

Orph said we should trust nature; that if we respected nature enough, it would see us through and help us to start again. We stopped talking about gods and angels and things like that. It had caused too much trouble, although when Orph came, people murmured that he was like an angel.

I wasn't born then, neither were my parents, but he was a part of our mythology and legend.

I was brought up on Orph stories; stories so strange and magical that sometimes I would ask, 'Was he really a human being?' He was attributed with such incredible gifts, such as singing, oratory and invention; but it was his gift of dowsing which had saved us all.

Of course, after the catastrophe and the drought which followed, dowsers and water diviners were more precious than gold; but there were many charlatans all out to make deals or buy time in their struggle for survival.

I remember how enthralled I was when I first heard the story of Orph, and how he turned up at our camp when my ancestors were on the brink of extinction. He was described as a thin child, not more than seven or eight, who had lost the power of speech. He was odd; more a wild animal than a human, who had hung about the outer edges of our settlement with a pack of dogs, scavenging alongside them for scraps and left-overs. His only possession was a mouth organ, which he played like a magician.

With it, he seemed to control beasts and humans alike. He was taken in out of pity, for it was assumed he was suffering from shock. But in time, in his dumb way, with signs, gestures and his mouth organ, he began to impart a clarity of vision and a depth of wisdom which made everyone take heed of him. An old teacher called him Orpheus, after some ancient Greek god who was a musician. Soon he became just Orph.

One day, after two years, Orph spoke. He stood on a rock in the middle of a barren, waterless place – my people had come there after a dreadful trek, during which scores had perished in an epidemic, and the rest had given up hope and were just waiting to die – and all he said was, 'I think I know where to go.' Then he began to sing, a strange, wordless, extraordinary song which rose high into falsetto in the upper regions of his throat, and then dropped down to a growl which rumbled round his stomach like a tiger's roar.

I wish I'd been there. My real father was told about it from his real father who had heard it. It could sound like the wind in a cave, or a spirit locked in a metal bowl or a ghost howling in the desert. It could be a low, liquid, cavernous sound, gushing fitfully out of his throat, or like the cry of an eagle soaring high on currents of air. And it could be like a floodgate burst open as he broke into a torrent of speech and song.

The people were so astounded, they just fell to their knees as if he were a god. He carried on in this way for four hours, then suddenly, he leapt down from the rock and flicked the ground with his divining stick. The rod jumped in his hands and began to tug him. It tugged so hard, that he had to run. The tribe ran after him. Even those who were sick and dying somehow struggled to their feet or dragged themselves along the ground on their bellies, desperate not to be left behind. He ran for an hour. Then abruptly, the stick becomes inanimate. Orph stopped as if felled by an axe and toppled headlong onto his stomach with exhaustion. The tribe gradually gathered around him, leaving a respectful distance, waiting for him to come to his senses. When he did, it was to tell them that he had found an underground river; that if they dug right there, they would find a small pool with enough clean water to sustain them for a few weeks, but that when everyone had their strength back, they must follow the underground river by means of his divining stick, and reach a safe place where they could settle for ever. Where they could build Athens again.

Yes, it was Orph who first talked of building Athens. No one knew how he knew about Athens. Many of the tribe had never heard of it and didn't know what he was talking about. But the same teacher who had named him Orpheus, who was now very old and close to death, explained it was the famous city state of Ancient Greece, from where our own civilization had once sprung, six or seven thousand years before the Great Drought.

His words were like a shaft of pure light. Despite all their dreadful hardship, this young boy spoke of hope and re-building and a future. So, of course, they followed him. They rushed around, gathering together what remnants of knowledge and technology were left, including some of the old weapons of warfare – just in case – and they carried it all as faithfully as the Israelites had carried the Ark of the Covenant.

They followed Orph for a year. They travelled along narrow valleys, they went into the mountains, edging through dangerous passes where cliff sides plunged for thousands of feet.

Many perished: some from accidents, cold or starvation, others suffering horribly from plague-like diseases. And the Arifi were all around them – ready to strike if they were ever off their guard.

One day, Orph left the tribe for a week. He told them he must lose the Arifi. No one knew how he did it. All he took was his mouth organ and dousing stick. Sometimes they thought they heard his voice carried on the wind. When he returned he said nothing and they struggled on. The Arifi never troubled us again while he was alive.

Then at last, one day, they reached a high plateau. In the centre of the plateau was a large lake, with an unfathomable depth, and here they stopped and set down the ark, and around this lake began to build Orph's dream city. A new Athens.

Only a small hard core of them had made it, but enough survived to form a viable community. My ancestors put seed into the ground; the farmers began to grow crops, the scientists to re-invent technology and the craftsmen to build. Despite their damaged bodies, they began having babies. By the time I was born fifty years later, I learned that we were a viable community with a developed city state that met all our needs.

'It is my belief that we should no longer fear the Arifi,' Navarth's voice was steady as she addressed the assembly. She rose from her chair to emphasize her meaning. 'We have our planet, Earth. It's perfectly big enough to sustain us all. If we do the right thing, more and more of it will recover. Look at our success. Look how we have extended the fertility of the land. We've replanted forests and meadows and cleaned up rivers. We should consider making links with the Arifi and help them to help themselves. We can't hold them back for ever. Sooner or later, they will come. Perdita is an illusion and can never develop beyond its own technology. Orph was right to reject it. Our future is here. We should stop being so afraid of outsiders.' Then she added. 'Let us face the Arifi and negotiate.'

Even Orph had never made such a suggestion.

The intake of breath was like the hissing of a vast serpent. What Navarth had said was like blasphemy. We have never made deals with any outsiders, let alone the Arifi. So no one was surprised when after the hubbub had died down, a citizen coldly ignored Navarth and tabled a motion. 'I propose we contact Perdita and ask for refugee status.'

It was like a slap in the face for Navarth. She sat pale and motionless as another voice cried, 'I second that!'

'Hear, hear!' The chamber exploded excitedly.

'They'll never take us all,' warned someone, and there was a groan.

Navarth spoke with composure. 'If that is your democratic wish, then you will have to draw lots, but the Law Lords must make the selection for the lottery, for Perdita will only allow the healthy on board. Those who are left can operate the Option if they wish – or stay with me in the city and face the Arifi.'

The groans faded to a long, thoughtful silence. The Option was to enter the Chamber of Hades, the great marble underground suicide chamber. It had been built for such an event, when it was thought better to die than to be taken by the Arifi.

Suddenly I was gripped by panic. So that was why! That was why Martin and Lara had made me put on a white tunic. I knew – I knew it was the garment of death.

Martin and Lara both had terminal illnesses – with not much more than a year or two to live. It was natural that they should want to opt for Hades. I turned to them, terror-stricken. 'Am I to die too?'

They put it to me that as I had a cancer I should consider the Hades Option, as the Law Lords would not allow anyone with a terminal illness to enter the lottery.

'But what about Rhett?' I cried. 'He can't be separated from me! He'll need me!'

'Rhett is young,' said Martin, 'and as yet totally free from disease. He is sure to be selected for Perdita if he wins in the lottery. Once on Perdita, he will be allocated a new family.'

'But I don't feel ready to die,' I cried and looked around to see if others felt like me.

'Better to die than fall into the hands of the Arifi,' came the response of those in white tunics.

Already people were selecting themselves, either for the lottery or for

Hades. I looked at Navarth. No one was coming to her. No one was prepared to stay.

Martin and Lara embraced Rhett and said they had loved him dearly. Then they tried to make me say 'goodbye' to him, but I refused. 'This feels wrong!' I cried. 'I'm not ready to die – and I'm not ready to leave Rhett. We'll stay with Navarth.'

'Would you deny Rhett the chance to live?' asked Martin softly. I felt his hand on my shoulder. His fingers tightened, and I knew that any moment now, he would hold me by force. Lara, on the other side, took my hand.

'Rhett!' I cried, shaking myself free and kneeling down to hug my brother. 'Rhett. Goodbye. I love you little brother. I hope they choose you for Perdita,' then suddenly I whirled him round and thrust him into my 'parents'. They were so startled that they lost their balance, and I fled from them. I thought I would never find my way out of the labyrinth. I twisted and turned until, in despair, I flung myself bodily against a wall. To my amazement, it was thin as a honeycomb, and I tumbled out into the open air. I was free. I ran and ran. I wanted to get as far away as possible from that assembly; away from Martin and Lara and the choices that they wanted us to make. Away from my little brother. 'Goodbye Rhett! I love you!' I screamed without looking back.

I didn't go home. I knew I had no home. No house, no street; no place anywhere in our enclave. I no longer belonged here. Our Athens was doomed.

Suddenly, all I wanted was the desert itself; to be out there – out, out, out in the world – whatever it cost me, whatever my fate. I wanted to be like the birds – like the hawk – soaring. I wanted freedom, if only for a brief moment.

'Wait for me! Wait for me!'

Rhett. I heard him wailing behind me. I stopped, but did not turn. I

waited for Rhett to catch up. I heard him panting up the slope and then his hot sweaty hand thrust into mine.

'Where are you going? Why did you leave me?'

I turned and looked down at him. The only living thing on this planet who shared my blood and genes and ancestry. 'Oh Rhett!' I threw my arms round him and held him tightly.

Perdita was gleaming like a white moon above the razor edges of the valley skyline.

'Look Rhett! There's Perdita. You could enter the lottery and have a chance of winning a place up there. You'd be safe. Safe from the Arifi and safe from the horrible diseases we all get here. You're healthy at the moment. No cancer, no allergies; nothing. Go in for the lottery, Rhett. Try and save yourself.'

I was crying as I spoke. Crying for the loneliness of the world; the loneliness of living with the unknown, the loneliness of our lost planet. Yet I wasn't without hope. I wasn't ready to die. I couldn't just give up. I wanted to possess every single last minute that was mine – good or bad, painful or calm. Death was the absolute and final end of everything. It was crazy to rush towards it so long as there was one scrap of air left to breathe.

A sound pierced my ears. A bird rose, flapping fiercely, its wings catching the last rays of a dying sun. It wheeled away, its cry echoing discordantly against a human voice which suddenly vibrated around us.

'I met an angel the other day.
He was made of water and blood and bone.
And skin and sinew and muscle
And iron and tin and zinc
And air and fire and earth
And liquid gold.'

I saw him; the troubadour. He was sitting just a few yards away, holding a stringed instrument close to his body as though it were another limb. There was nothing sharp about him. I stared at his face – with skin like the skin of a drum, taut, stretched, from neck to shoulder and elbow to wrist and waist to thigh and legs to ankles. Yet his frame seemed rounded and shaped and moulded as if he had been cast in golden sand.

When the song ended, he turned and looked at us with the clearest blue eyes I had ever seen.

Rhett left my side and ran to him as naturally as a lamb to its shepherd.

'You live out there?' I called to the troubadour, waving my hand beyond the plateau to the desert plains below.

'Yes.'

'And you're going there now? Down there, where there might be the Arifi?'

Even as I spoke I heard the whistle of the desert wind, and felt grains of sand scalding my cheeks.

'I am an Arifi.'

Rhett didn't move. Neither did I. We just stood there staring.

The troubadour rose and held the bow of his instrument before him.

'Are you a dowser?' It was Rhett who spoke first. 'Like Orph?'

'Yes. I only go where my bow leads me.' The troubadour held his bow in front of him. I saw it spring and swivel in his hands, and with a tug, seemed to turn him towards a track barely wide enough for a goat.

'Was Orph an Arifi?' I asked.

The troubadour shrugged. 'He came from the desert as you did once.' He patted Rhett on the head. 'I just sing, that's all, and I follow my bow.'

The bow quivered and pulled him. Tucking his instrument under his arm, he began the descent, following the track which twisted away between high rocks and boulders at the head of the canyon. Below, the darkness gathered. He raised his hand – to say goodbye, or was it as a guide, to wave us on? He began to sing. I could hear his voice throbbing through the caves. Now I knew how Orph must have sounded.

The shadows enveloped him. Rhett came silently to my side and took my hand.

'I'm going where he's going' I said, without looking at my brother.

'Good,' he said simply. 'You lead. I'll follow.'

As I set off, I heard Rhett skipping behind me. He was humming in harmony with the troubadour's song. After a while, his hum burst through his open mouth in a shrill boy's treble.

> 'And when he sang, his voice
> Like pinprick stars
> Pierced the heaven of my heart.
> And when he sang, notes
> Hollow and dark
> From subterranean depths
> Shuddered, when he sang.
>
> I met an angel the other day
> Whose feet were on the ground.
> I was flying
> Flying
> Flying.'

The Wobby Gurgle

PAUL JENNINGS

Illustrated by Louise Brierley

 A PERSON who eats someone is called a cannibal. But what are you called if you drink someone? Like I did.

No, no, no. Don't put down the book. This isn't a horror story. It isn't even a horrible story. And it's not about vampires and ghouls. But it sure is a weird tale. Really weird.

Now you can say that you don't believe me if you like. But I tell you this – I don't tell lies. Well, that's not quite true. I did tell one once. A real big one. Did I do the right thing? I don't know. You be the judge.

It began the day Dad and I moved to the end of the world.

There we were. In the middle of the desert. The proud new owners of the Blue Singlet Motel. There was no school. There was no post office. There was no pub. There were no other kids. There was nothing except us and our little café with its petrol pumps. And two rooms out the back for rent.

The red desert stretched off in every direction.

And it was hot. Boy, was it hot. The heat shimmered up off the sand. When you walked outside you could feel the soles of your shoes cooking.

'Paradise,' said Dad. 'Don't you reckon?'

'Ten million flies can't be wrong,' I said, waving a couple of hundred of them away from my face.

'Don't be so gloomy,' said Dad. 'You'll love it. The trucks all stop here on their way to Perth. It's a little goldmine.'

Just then I noticed the dust stirring in the distance. 'Our first customer,' said Dad. A huge truck was buzzing towards us at great speed. Dad picked up the nozzle of the petrol pump. 'He'll probably want about a hundred litres,' he said with a grin.

The truck roared down the road. And kept roaring. Straight past. It vanished into the lonely desert. Poor old Dad's face fell. He put the nozzle back on the pump. Don't worry,' he said. 'There'll be plenty of others.'

But he was wrong. For some reason hardly any of the trucks pulled up. They just tore on by. There were a few tourists. They stopped and bought maps and filled up their water-bottles and topped up with petrol. Some even stayed the night. It was a living. But it wasn't a goldmine.

But to be honest it wasn't too bad. And Dad had a plan. A plan to attract customers.

'It's called a Wobby Gurgle,' Dad said, waving an old faded book at me. 'There's a legend that the Wobby Gurgle lives around here in the desert.'

'What's it look like?' I said.

Dad looked a bit embarrassed. 'No one's ever seen one,' he said.

'Well, how do you know there's any such thing?'

'Stories,' said Dad. 'There are stories.'

'Well, what does a Wobby Gurgle do?' I asked.

'Drink.'

'Drink?'

'Yes,' he went on. 'It, ah, likes to drink water.'

I scoffed. 'There isn't any water around here. Only what we bring in by truck. There isn't a water hole for hundreds of miles.'

Dad wasn't going to give up. 'Well, maybe it sort of saves water up. Like a camel.'

'It would have to be big. It hasn't rained here for twelve years,' I told him.

Dad tried to shush me up, he was getting all excited. 'Imagine if it was true,' he said. 'People would come from everywhere to see it. We could sell films and souvenirs. Lots of petrol. We could open a museum. Or a pub.'

Dad was getting excited. His face was one big happy grin.

'Like the Loch Ness Monster,' he yelped. 'No one's ever really seen it. But people go to Loch Ness from all over the world – just hoping to catch a glimpse.'

'So?' I said.

'So we let people know about the Wobby Gurgle. They'll come for miles to see it.'

'But what if there isn't one?' I said. 'Then you would be telling a lie.'

Dad's face fell. 'I know,' he said. 'But we'll keep our eyes open. If we see one it will be like hitting the jackpot.'

Well, we didn't see anything. Not for a long time anyway. Time passed and I started to enjoy living at the Blue Singlet Motel. We didn't make a lot of money. But we got by.

I liked the evenings best. After the sun went down and the desert started to cool. Sometimes a gentle breeze would blow in the window. I would sit there staring into the silent desert, wondering if anything was out there.

'Never go anywhere without a water-bottle,' Dad used to say. 'You never know what can happen out here in the desert.'

Anyway, this is about the time that things started to get weird. One night I filled my water-bottle to the brim and put it on the window-sill as usual. I fell off to sleep quickly. But something was wrong. I had bad dreams. About waterfalls. And tidal waves. And flooding rivers.

I was drowning in a huge river. I gave a scream and woke up with a start. I was thirsty. My throat was parched and dry. I went over to my water-bottle and opened it.

Half the water was gone.

I examined it for holes. None.

Who would do such a thing? Dad was the only other person around and I could hear him snoring away in his bedroom. He would never pinch my water. He was the one always giving me a lecture about never leaving the property without it.

I looked at the ground outside. My heart stopped. There on the still-warm sand, was a wet footprint.

I opened my mouth to call out for Dad. But something made me stop. I just had the feeling that I should handle this myself. It was a strange sensation. I was scared but I didn't tell Dad.

I jumped out of the window and bent over the footprint. I touched it gently with one finger.

Pow. A little zap ran up my arm. It didn't hurt but it gave me a fright. It was like the feeling you get when lemonade bubbles fizz up your nose. Like that but all over.

I jumped back and looked around nervously. The night was dark. The moon had not yet risen. All around me the endless desert spread itself to the edges of the world.

The warm sand seemed to call me. I took a few steps and discovered another footprint. And another. A line of wet footprints led off into the blackness.

I wanted to go home. Turn and run back to safety. But I followed the trail, still clutching the half-empty water-bottle in my hand.

How could someone have wet feet in the desert? There was no pond. No spring. No creek. Just the endless red sand.

The footprints followed the easiest way to walk. They avoided rocks and sharp grasses. On they went. And on.

I was frightened. My legs were shaking. But I had to know who or what had made these prints. I was sure that a Wobby Gurgle had gone this way.

I could run and get Dad, but the trail would have vanished by then. The tracks behind me were evaporating. In a few minutes there would be no trail to follow.

If I could find a Wobby Gurgle we would be set. Visitors would come by the thousand.

A cricket chirped as I hurried on. A night mouse scampered out of my way. Soon the café was only a dark shadow in the distance. Should I go on? Or should I go back?

I knew the answer.

I had to go back. It was the sensible thing to do. Otherwise I might be gobbled up by the desert. I was in my pyjamas and slippers. And only had half a bottle of water. That wouldn't last long. Not once the sun came up.

The footprints were fading fast. I looked back at the café. Then I headed off in the opposite direction, following the tracks into the wilderness.

I had never been one to do the sensible thing. And anyway, if I could spot a Wobby Gurgle we would make a fortune. Tourists would come from everywhere to look for it. That's what kept me going.

On I went and on. The moon rose high in the sky and turned the sand to silver. The Blue Singlet Motel vanished behind me. I was alone with the wet footprints. And an unknown creature of the night.

The moon started to lower itself into the inky distance. Soon the sun would bleach the black sky. And dry the footprints as quickly as they were made. I had to hurry.

My eyes scoured the distance. Was that a silvery figure ahead? Or just the moon playing tricks?

It was a tree. A gnarled old tree, barely clinging to life on the arid plains. I was disappointed but also a little relieved. I wasn't really sure that I wanted to find anything.

I decided to climb the tree. I would be able to see far ahead. If there was nothing there I would turn around and go home. I grabbed the lowest branch of the tree.

I can't quite remember who saw what first.

The creature or me.

I couldn't make any sense of it. My mind wouldn't take it in. At first I thought it was a man made of jelly. It seemed to walk with wobbly steps. It was silvery and had no clothes on.

It let out a scream. No, not a scream. A gurgle. Well, not a gurgle either. I guess you could call it a scurgle. A terrifying glugging noise. Like someone had pulled out a bath plug in its throat.

It was me that let out a scream. Boy, did I yell. Then I turned and raced off into the night. I didn't know where I was running. What I was doing. I stumbled and jumped and ran. I felt as if any moment a silvery hand was going to reach out and drag me back. Eat me up.

But it didn't. Finally I fell to the ground, panting. I couldn't have moved another step, even if I'd wanted to. I looked fearfully behind me. But there was nothing. Only the first rays of the new day in the morning sky.

Soon it would be hot. Unbearably hot. I stood up and staggered on towards where I thought the Blue Singlet Motel should be.

I wandered on and on. The sun rose in the sky and glared down on me. As I went a change came over me. My fear of the Wobby Gurgle started to fade. And be replaced by another terror. Death in the desert. I was hopelessly lost.

The water-bottle was warm in my hand. I raised it to my lips and took a sip. I had to make it last.

By now my face was burning. Flies buzzed in my eyes. My mouth felt as if I had eaten sand for breakfast. My slippered feet were like coals of fire. My breath was as dry as a dragon's dinner.

Stupid, stupid, stupid. To leave home in the middle of the night. With only a little water. And no hat. Dressed in pyjamas. The heat was sending me crazy.

How long I walked for I couldn't say. Maybe hours. Maybe days. My throat screamed for water. In the end I guzzled the lot in one go. I was going mad with thirst.

I laughed crazily. 'Wobby Gurgle,' I shouted. 'Come and get me. See if I care.'

Finally I stumbled upon a small burrow under a rock. There was just enough room for me to curl up in its shade. I knew that without help I would never leave that spot.

Night fell. I dozed. And dreamed. And swallowed with a tongue that was cracked and dry. I dreamed of water. Sweet water. I was in a cool, cool place. A wet hand was stroking my face. A lovely damp hand, fresh from a mountain stream.

I opened my eyes.

It wasn't a dream.

Or a nightmare.

It was the Wobby Gurgle.

Normally I would have screamed and ran. But in my near-dead state I only smiled. Smiled as if it was perfectly normal to see a man made of water.

He had no bones. No blood. No muscles. His skin was like clear plastic. The nearest image I can think of is a balloon filled with water. But a balloon shaped like a man. With arms and legs and fingers. All made of water.

For a silly second I wondered what would happen if I stuck a pin in him. Would he collapse in a shower and seep away into the sand?

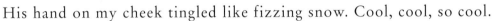

His water lips smiled sadly. His hand on my cheek tingled like fizzing snow. Cool, cool, so cool.

Inside his chest a tiny, dark red fish circled lazily. I knew that I must be losing my mind. There is no such thing as a man made of water. With a fish swimming inside him.

It was then that he did the weirdest thing of all. He placed the end of one finger into my mouth. It was cold and fresh and filled me with sparkling freshness. A little electric shock ran all over me.

I felt a trickle of pure water on my tongue. The clearest, coolest, freshest water in the world. I sucked like a calf at a teat. The Wobby Gurgle was feeding me. With himself.

The freshness was so good. I was greedy. I swallowed until I could take no more.

'Thanks,' I managed to croak.

He didn't answer. Well, not in speaking. He just gave me a gentle gurgle. Like a mountain stream trickling over a rock.

He stood up and started to move off. 'Don't leave me,' I said. 'Don't go.'

The Wobby Gurgle looked up at the sky. The sun was already rising. I had to get home that night. Another day in the desert would finish me.

And him? Would it finish him too? Where did he live? In a cool burrow somewhere? I didn't know. But I remembered Dad's words. Maybe he stored up water like a camel. Maybe he was carrying twelve years' supply.

I staggered after him, somehow realizing that he was leading me in the right direction. Every now and then he would give a low gurgle, as if to encourage me.

The sun beat down mercilessly. I wondered how he could stand it. My throat was dry. I wanted water. But I didn't like to ask. I knew I would never make it without regular drinks.

So did the Wobby Gurgle. He seemed to know when I couldn't go on. Every fifteen minutes or so he would come and put his cool finger into my mouth. And I would feel the trickle of fizzing liquid flowing across my tongue.

He was so gentle. So generous. Waiting. Leading me on. Giving me a drink. Pure, pure water.

After several hours I felt much stronger. But the Wobby Gurgle seemed to be moving more slowly. His steps were shorter. And was it my imagination or had he shrunk?

On he went. On and on. With the cruel sun beating down. We stopped more often for a drink and after each one the Wobby Gurgle walked more slowly.

I looked at him carefully. The tiny fish seemed bigger as it floated effortlesly inside his arm. It wasn't bigger. He was smaller.

I was drinking him.

'No,' I screamed. 'No. I can't do it. You're killing yourself for me. You'll soon be empty.'

He seemed to smile. If a water face can smile.

Once again he placed his finger in my mouth. And like a greedy baby at its mother's breast I sucked and swallowed.

The day wore on and the Wobby Gurgle grew smaller and smaller with every drink. I clamped my jaw shut. I refused to open my mouth. I wasn't going to let him kill himself for me. No way.

But it was no use. He simply pointed at my mouth and let fly with a jet of water. It ran down my chin and dripped onto the dry sand, wasted. He wasn't going to stop until I swallowed. I opened my mouth and accepted the gift of life.

As the afternoon wore away, so did the Wobby Gurgle. By now he was only half my size. A little bag of liquid. His steps were small and slow. Like an exhausted child.

I tried to stop him feeding me. But it was no good, he simply poured himself onto my face if I refused.

In the end he was no bigger than my fist. A small figure, wearily leading me on at a snail's pace. I picked him up in one hand and looked at him. The fish almost totally filled his body. He held no more than a few cupfuls of water.

'That's it,' I said. 'I'm not taking any more. I'd sooner die myself. If you give me any more I'll run off. You'll never catch me.'

He looked up sadly. He knew that he was beaten.

And so was I.

The sun set once again. And the far-off moon, unknowing, uncaring, rose in the night sky.

I thought that I could last until morning. But the tiny Wobby Gurgle, how long could he last?

We both fell asleep. Me and my little friend – the bag of water.

Later, I woke and with a fright saw that the Wobby Gurgle was lying on his back, not moving. The dark red fish inside him floated upside down.

'Hey,' I yelled, 'wake up.'

There was no movement. He looked like a tiny, clear football that had been emptied of air. I knew he was dying.

Tears trickled down my cheek. How I had enough moisture to make tears I will never know. I was so filled with sorrow that I didn't see the watcher. The sad, silent watcher.

A woman. A water woman. With a gasp I saw her out of the corner of my eye. She seemed to flow across the desert sand rather than walk.

'Quick,' I yelled. 'Here.'

I pointed to the tiny, deflated figure on the sand.

She didn't look at me but just bent over the still figure and gently kissed him on his water lips.

It was the most beautiful sight I had ever seen. Water flowed from her lips into his. She was filling him up. From herself. It was like watching a tyre being inflated. He grew larger and she grew smaller. The fish once more began to swim. The kiss of life went on and on until both Wobby Gurgles were the same size. About my size. Three kids in the desert.

Well, no. One kid. And two wonderful half empty Wobby Gurgles.

They both smiled. So gently. Then the woman held out her water-filled arm and pointed. In the distance I could see a red glow. It was the neon light of the Blue Singlet Motel.

'Thanks,' I yelled. It seemed such a small thing to say. I could never repay them for what they had done. I turned around to try and tell them how I felt.

But they had both gone. I was alone in the night. I walked towards home. As I got closer I could see the police cars. And the search helicopter. Dad would have lots of customers.

But not as many as he would have when the word about the Wobby Gurgles got out.

People made of water.

Visitors would come from everywhere. Australians. Americans. Japanese. Germans. Clicking their cameras. Buying their films. There would be museums. Hotels. Pizza parlours. Probably even poker machines. We would be famous. And rich.

Dad came rushing out with tears streaming down his face. He hugged me until I couldn't breathe.

'How did you stay alive?' he said. 'With no water? Did someone help you?'

I looked at him for a long time. The police were listening – everyone wanted to know what had happened. I thought about the Wobby Gurgles. Those shy, generous people. Who had given the water of life to a greedy boy. Then I thought about the crowds with the cameras. And the noise and the pizza shops that would follow.

I thought about all the plants and the flowers that had vanished from this country for ever.

'Well?' said Dad.

He was a good dad. But I knew that he would want to find the Wobby Gurgles. That's when I looked at him and told a lie.

'No,' I said. 'I never saw anyone.'

Did I do the right thing? You be the judge.

In a House Built Out of Dragonfly Wings

TIM WYNNE-JONES

Illustrated by PJ Lynch

THERE IS an overgrown trail off the Foxtail Road that leads down through maple and silver birch to a brook. It is an old logging trail, but Jess calls it the Haunted Road and she calls the brook the Stream of Dreams. She says there is a tiny house on a rock below the Teacup Falls. The house is really a jail, she says, and it's made out of dragonfly wings and there is a girl, who was kidnapped by the gremlins, trapped inside it.

'Does your guitar really have strings made of cat's guts?' she asks Walker.

Walker shakes his head. 'Nylon,' he says. She glares, chooses not to believe him.

'Well, I think the door of the dragonfly house is made out of cat-gut strings, anyway, but they are enchanted so that the girl inside can't get through them. When she rattles her cage it sounds kind of pretty, though. For a prison.'

On and on, Jess rattles. And Walker listens and Walker hears about as much as any eighteen-year-old ever does a ten-year-old.

He knows the brook, the Teacup Falls, though it had always been just 'the falls' to him. Lying on the bank there on a spring day, not unlike this one, when he was about Jess's age he watched an otter cruise downstream towards him. He recalls it vividly now. He remembers knowing even then with all the certainty of childhood that the otter was playing. Not hunting, not building a den or on the make – not working. Playing.

He used that otter once in an argument with his father.

'Animals don't play,' his father told him with all the certainty of adulthood. Then he issued Walker a dire warning. 'Let me tell you this, my friend; no wild animal dies of old age.'

Walker wasn't sure what he meant. But his father had rhymed it off as if it were the *coup de grace* in their quarrel. It was only later that Walker learned it wasn't his father's idea, anyway; it was a quote from Earnest Thompson Seaton whose nature stories were almost as dreary as was his father.

He remembers that quarrel now and thinks of how little play there was in his father. Maybe that was the reason his mother divorced him. Then Walker thinks of play and wonders how much of it there is in his own life at college. His guitar, of course; weekend parties, beer, girls. But even that seems like work, sometimes. Has he died then, the child in him?

Gleefully, he recalls the otter, how it came *that* close to where he lay in wait, hardly breathing, before it noticed him and fled overland in terror. But he doesn't recall any dragonfly real estate. He was never that kind of a kid.

Walker is tagging along not for the fairy house but because it is spring. Spring is his agenda; and that long-ago otter, bright again in his mind's eye, poking its whiskery nose up through the residue of study books and exam papers littering the floor of his exhausted brain.

Wild leeks are on his agenda, too. There were leeks up this way; sharp, green shoots in the wadded carpet of the forest floor.

And finally, there is Jess. It has been a rough term and Jess is powerful medicine.

The moon shines foolishly in the middle of the afternoon sky.

'Do you think there could be something like derring don't?' asks Jess. 'Kind of the opposite of derring do.'

Walker is amused. 'Derring don't? Why not. Someone filled with the desire *not* to do anything adventurous?'

'Yeah,' says Jess. 'That's exactly what I was thinking.'

'Then how about free won't?' says Walker, caught up in Jess's enthusiasm, for everything under the frail thumb print of a moon. 'I guess that would be the freedom to *not* be able to do what you want to do.'

Side by side, Jess and Walker slog through the sodden leaves, eviscerated of colour by the winter. 'Are you thinking about your princess in her dragonfly jail?' he asks.

'She's not a princess, Walk, just a girl. And I wasn't thinking about her, just now. I was trying to think what free won't is. Is it the opposite of free will? Is that the joke? Because I don't know what free will is.'

Walker chuckles to himself. To explain free will to Jess would be like explaining how to get home to Lassie. 'How do we get in these conversations, Jess?'

Jess shrugs. 'I guess it's because I was talking about derring do and derring don't but I can't remember why, any more.'

'Oh,' says Walker. And then he stops and says, 'Shhh.' For the sound of the brook has come to him.

They are quiet: Jess with the hope of catching gremlins at work; Walker with the hope of catching otters at play.

There are rocks, a careless stairway down into the Teacup. Silently Walker and Jess make their way to where the brook, having splashed through an obstacle course of boulders and dead trees, cascades down a series of rapids and pools to the swampy, wooded valley below.

And because they are so diligent in their silence, they hear a sound above the noise of splashing water that is neither fairy folk nor anything quite natural. A metal creaking, a clanking sound. A man's laugh. Jess skibbles back up to the rim of the Teacup, Walker follows awkwardly on all fours.

Down below and only a stone's throw away through the still-naked trees, stands a half-ton truck, its back to them, its body sprung high for off-road sport. There are two men standing on the tailgate tipping a forty-gallon drum. A thick stream of black sludge gushes out onto the ground. There are four drums in all.

'What the hell!' says Walker.

'We have to get their licence plate number,' whispers Jess. Walker nods in agreement and starts to calculate in his mind whether the men have just started or whether they're just finishing; whether he and Jess can make it back through the woods in time to intercept the vehicle out on the open road; whether they can make it look unintentional; whether he has a pencil.

Jess, however, is untroubled by strategy. She's up over the lip of the Teacup and skibbling down the hill towards the men, darting, stumbling – half falling – from tree to tree. Walker prepares for trouble.

But it doesn't come. The men finish their business, wipe their hands on their grimy overalls, oblivious to the witness of their crime. The engine roars and the truck lurches up what must be another logging trail, for these woods were logged heavily in the old days. The truck's wheels spin in the mud, with no load any longer, over the back tyres. By the time Walker joins Jess, she's writing the licence plate number with a rock on the slimy backside of a piece of birch bark.

'Nice work,' says Walker. He wants to scold her for her rashness, but he stops himself. He doesn't want to be accused of derring don't.

She hands him the birch bark evidence and looks anywhere but at the oil spill.

'Neat, eh!' she says. And Walker notices for the first time they are standing in an old junk yard, an abandoned dump site on the edge of swampy ground. He can't remember ever knowing it was there before. Jess seems delighted. There are bedsprings, and bowed pieces of ancient farm equipment. There is a refrigerator with its doors torn off, and a cracked wood stove with weeds growing in the firebox like newly-minted flames.

It is an old dump, its rusty feet still trapped in hard grey snow. It is overgrown. There are no coke cans, no plastics. Nothing new but a small lake of black effluent.

Jess explores. She liberates a steering wheel and drives it around the dump. She tries on a tractor seat as if it were the latest in spring helmets. Walker stands on the shore of the inky sludge feeling somehow abandoned.

'Look at this!' cries Jess. She has found the carcass of a telephone booth. 'This must be pre-Columbian,' she says, for Columbus has figured prominently in her schoolwork this term.

She kneels down and picks through broken glass and drags out a matted coat of animal pelts. 'No, it's older,' she says. 'Probably Stone Age. Look at this, Walk, look. There's a label inside the collar. "Property of Og the Caveman".'

Walker cannot speak. It is shady down here, colder. All the spring seems to have been wrung out of the day.

'Maybe he was phoning home,' Jess rattles on, 'to tell Ogetta that the woolly mammoth hunt wasn't going so well when – Boom! – he was hit by a meteorite.'

'Boom!' says Walker. 'Bloody boom . . .'

Jess makes a face at him, at his apparent bad mood. She slips her arm into one of the coat's tattered sleeves. She is tentative, fearing perhaps, that her fingers might make contact with some of Og, or a mouse, or a slug family. Triumphantly, her fist pokes through the opening. Then fearlessly, her left arm navigates the damp reaches of the other sleeve.

'This used to be a whole herd of raccoons,' she says. 'Imagine.'

'Do you have any idea what vermin probably live in that thing, now?' says Walker.

Jess looks down at the tattered hem hanging around her ankles. She sniffs. 'It stinks,' she says, but makes no move to take it off. Then she has to skip-step aside, for a rivulet of the oily puddle has found its way to her.

'What is it?' she asks, wrinkling her nose.

'Gunk,' says Walker. 'Lubricant soup. Crank case oil, goop of all kinds – you name it.'

Jess joins Walker beside the still, dark pond. She growls, 'The devil damn those cream-faced loons!'

The sun is low on Foxtail Road. Jess spins around to make her new-old coat twirl. It is so heavy she almost falls over. 'I think it belongs to Superman,' she says.

'What happened to Og?'

Jess snorts. 'Oh come on, Walk. As if they had phones in the Stone Age.'

But Walker doesn't rise to the bait. He is filled with chagrin. And Jess's gaiety annoys him.

'You know how he changes in phone booths?' she says. 'Well, he must have left it there, see.'

'Sure,' says Walker. 'Right.'

Jess is Walker's step-sister, his mother's other kid. His father never remarried. Too busy. Their mother is away, right now. She is an actress. She is playing Lady Macbeth in Winnipeg. That's where the 'cream-faced loons' came from. Macbeth. Jess has learned all the lines. There was even a chance she'd get to play MacDuff's son but the director's nephew got the part. She would have loved it. 'Thou li'st thou shag ear'd villain!' She is not a child of ordinary curses.

Jess's' father, Steve, phones the police, when they tell him what they've seen. The police tell Steve it's not in their jurisdiction; they should phone the provincial police. The provincial police tell him to phone the offices of the municipality. But the offices are closed. 'I'll phone first thing in the morning,' says Steve.

Jess sits on the kitchen floor in Superman's discarded furs, absorbed in getting her barbie doll into a fur coat of her own. She pushes too hard, tears one of Barbie's sleeves.

'Hell-Kite,' she says.

'Jess!' says Steve. 'And will you *please* get that wretched coat out of the house.'

Walker dreams of an otter. There is no one lying in wait; no one to scare it off. It is his dream but he is not in it. Suddenly the otter pricks up its ears, listens, scampers out of the stream, terrified. By what, what? Then Walker is sitting up in bed, falling out of bed, his feet tied up in the bed clothes. Someone is screaming.

It's not a dream. It's Jess. Her father is the first to reach her.

'O, O, O,' she sobs, wringing her hands. She trembles in his arms. 'Everything will be black,' she says. 'The girl, the girl. She's trapped.'

'I'll get you a glass of water,' says Walker. When he arrives back, Jess is a bit calmer but disoriented. She takes the glass from him but stares at it suspiciously. 'Won't drink it. Won't.'

'What are we going to do, Walk?' she says, her voice small and pleading. 'The goop will be all gone by the time anyone bothers to go see it.'

Walker sighs. 'I'll go get a jar of it, okay? As evidence.'

'Okay.'

'First thing tomorrow.'

'No. Now.'

'It's midnight, Jess. Tomorrow. First thing.'

'No, no, no!' says Jess. Suddenly she's out of bed and heading for the door, fighting off all attempts to restrain her. Walker and her father block the way. She is out of control. No pleading, no sweet language will contain her. Around and around her room she tromps, over the bed, down the other side, urgent, unmanageable.

She has sneaked the raggedy coat up to her room. Now she slips it on. She points her finger at her two pursuers, stopping them in their tracks.

'This is Superman's coat!' she warns them. She is shaking with rage. Then – maybe it's the looks on their faces, or maybe she has only just woken up – suddenly it's too funny and she is laughing. Then crying. Then they are holding her.

Then somehow, though he cannot quite believe he agreed to it, Walker is out in the blustery spring night, in boots and a winter parka, with a flashlight and an empty Miracle Whip bottle on a goop-gathering mission.

The moon – confused by spring – set before nightfall. There is only starlight to accompany Walker on his lonely mission. Stars and the wind in the pines and the spring peepers in the lowland. And a barred owl barking like a moonthroated dog.

His mind is full of Jess wringing her hands, like Lady Macbeth; sleep-walking, unable to wash away the blood stains from her own murderous hands. This is not a comforting thought.

And it's a great deal worse when Walker veers off the Foxtail Road into the woods, the closer darkness of the Haunted Road. He curses Jess and her fertile imagination – her naming of things – for it has infected him.

Things move in the woods, creak, and snap, stirred by the wind. Things skitter for shelter, stalked by night hunters. Branches break under foot, or reach out and brush his cheek with alarming familiarity. Even the sound of Teacup Falls, when it comes to him at last, holds little pleasure. It is too loud, covers up too much else. Walker finds himself flinging the flimsy beam of his flashlight every which way, manufacturing monsters in the tangle of shadows and wind-fingered undergrowth. A bear. Wolves. Three witches. Two men in overalls with oil-dirty hands.

Here are his and Jess's tracks from the afternoon, sinking into the boggy ground along the stream's bank. Down the rocky steps, below the wind, into the sheltered dip of land Jess calls the Teacup.

From here he will make his way down to the valley floor and the dump. He just needs a little rest before making his descent. He sits on a boulder by the brook, trying to collect his racing thoughts. He shivers, for this moonless April night is still fat with winter.

A clattering sound comes to him from farther down the stream. He stops a raccoon in his flashlight's beam.

It is perched on a table rock which juts out over the falling water. One paw is deep inside something which looks to Walker at first glance like a hive of some kind but which glitters faintly in the light. The raccoon is transfixed by the beam. Then hastily it withdraws its paw, something white in its grasp.

'Shoo!' whispers Walker. And the raccoon jumps down from the rock, dropping whatever it has won from the hive-like thing, and races off into the forest.

Walker tracks the raccoon with his flashlight until it is out of sight, then he swings his beam back to the construction on the rock. It is not a hive but an inverted bowl-shaped thing.

Walker slides down the bank on the seat of his pants. The scent of wild leeks rises up around him. Finally he stops beside a small mystery, a dome-shaped creation. The structure sways in a gust of wind. Impulsively, Walker reaches out to catch it, fearing it will be whisked clear off its foundation, whirled away into the night. But it is fixed to the rock. There is a tear in its side where the raccoon has been at work. Caught in the rocks at the foot of the stone table Walker finds a small white naked doll.

He peers closer at the construct. It is made, it seems, entirely from dragonfly wings. Bending low, so that his chin hovers just above the cold granite table, Walker shines his light through the transparent walls. There is a bed made of twigs tied together with woven grass. The bed is weighted down with a beautiful rounded stone pillow. There is a handkerchief bedspread half dragged off the little bed onto the floor of the dragonfly house. With each gust of wind the house seems to breathe. In and out. So fragile and yet so strong.

Walker's fears desert him. He is filled with astonishment, with wonder. He hunkers down close to the rock out of the wind. He remembers how every year the dragonflies come. Their coming is a celebration for it marks the end of blackfly season. The dragonflies are the cavalry of early summer. Whirlybird knights. They come in scores, gobbling blackflies by day and resting on the west wall of the house in the evening, as if recharging their batteries in the setting sun.

The dragonfly is Jess's totem, thinks Walker, her spirit animal. When they are killed, as many of them are, by passing cars, Jess picks up their broken bodies from along the Foxtail Road; and she plucks them off the car grills and out of the mesh of screen doors and windows. She collects them in a blue and emerald green pottery bowl. He has seen it on her window-sill. And now she has built this house, though how she has accomplished it, Walker cannot tell.

Another gust of wind smacks the gossamer walls. It wobbles but does not fly apart as Walker fears it must. It just breathes quietly, in and out like a sleeping mouth. Walker looks closely at the tiny doll-baby in his palm, pockets it. Then he sees that the raccoon has left something behind; oily paw prints on the table rock. With new resolve, he makes his way down to the dump. He manages to fill most of the bottle with goop-soaked earth.

The Municipal Offices tell them to phone the Ministry of the Environment and Energy who refer them to the special Environmental Spill number who say they'll look into it. And they do. The investigator even drops around to report. The licence plate number belongs to a vehicle owned by an automobile establishment. The investigator cannot divulge the owner's name, but he has visited the establishment.

'They're properly registered,' he says. 'They've got what's called a waste generator number,' he says. 'That means they are required by law to have all hazardous waste removed by a licensed company. They have a receipt of a pick-up on Tuesday. They're too small an operation to have produced even a single drum of waste since then, let alone four,' he says.

Jess scowls at the investigator. 'Well, they did!'

'That may be so,' says the investigator. 'But it seems the owner is plagued by youths trespassing on his property, playing in his wrecking yard. Stealing things. He's had to run them off quite a few times and he seems to think there are a few of those kids who wouldn't mind making things hot for him, if they had the chance.'

It takes Walker a moment to digest this news, pick up on the inference. 'We're not making this up,' he says. 'You saw the spill yourself.'

The investigator shrugs. 'I did. And I believe what you're telling me. But the fine for this kind of illegal dumping is pretty steep. If we try to prosecute, this guy is going to claim it's all a frame-up. We've only got circumstantial evidence. It's his word against yours.

'If you could get photographs then we'd have something to work with,' says the investigator. He asks them to keep their eyes open. Then he's gone.

'Hell-kite!' says Jess.

'Now, now,' says Steve. 'He's done what he can.'

'I didn't mean him,' says Jess, 'I mean Merkley's Auto Wrecking.'

Walker and Steve stare at her, mouths agape.

'Well, that's who he's talking about,' says Jess.

And so the story unfolds a bit more. Jess had recognized the men making the dump when she saw them up close. She'd recognized the truck, too. They work for Merkley's Auto Wrecking up on the French Line.

'We go there sometimes after school,' she says. 'They've never caught me, though. And we *don't* steal stuff!' she says. 'We just play freedom-fighters in the dead cars. It's just a game.'

Then, before anyone can say anything adultish, she heads for her room. 'It's not as if we were killing anyone,' she says.

Walker isn't sure what to do and so he does nothing. There are summer job interviews to go to and old school friends to visit. There are errands to run and a left-over paper to write for school. And there is Jess to visit with and baby-sit when Steve's away. They play cards at night, Spite & Malice. She is merciless.

What Walker doesn't know, because Jess doesn't tell him, is that she has declared a personal war on Merkley's Auto Wrecking. She is a warrior for the Stream of Dreams.

She bikes up to Merkley's every day after school. She stands in full view of the office window in her invincible Superman coat until Merkley yells at her to vamoose. Then she crosses the road and marches back and forth in front of his property or plays provocatively with the flap on his mail box until he yells some more.

She makes a sandwich board. 'Looking for a large oil spill?' it says on the front. Then on the back it says, 'Just call Merkley for free home delivery.'

'I'm calling the cops,' Merkley bawls at her.

'Good,' she says.

But he doesn't.

Then she enlists some willing friends. They play the wrecking yard as if it were a great noisy instrument of torture. They pull out all the stops. They bang on wrecked car doors and yodel through improvised megaphones. Kid's stuff.

Merkley and his men chase them away.

She steals out of bed one night and spray-paints his office window. 'Environment Killer.'

She prints up a flyer spelling out Merkley's crime in detail. She and her friends deliver it all over the neighbourhood. That's when Merkley really does call the cops. Jess is there waiting for them. The cop bends Jess's ear. He drives her home. Walker is the only one there, right then. The cop tells Walker what she's been up to. He tells Walker to have Jess's father contact him. He issues her a dire warning.

'Shag ear'd villain,' she says, when the cop car leaves.

And Walker is terribly proud of Jess and terribly sad. Because, to his mind, it is not a game anymore. Among his sins, Merkley has stolen Jess's childhood. That's what Walker thinks and he burns with frustration. But he is wrong, about Jess. She is playing hard, devoted to her game. He worries. He thinks of Jess's miraculous house by the Teacup Falls and he wishes his mother were home. Jess is so like her. And he is not. He is not.

Jess goes underground. She spies, lurks, prowls, slinks, skulks and glides between the rusting hulks of Merkley's wrecked kingdom. She sees a truck come to take away Merkley's hazardous waste, pumping it up from a holding tank. But there is goop and gunk the licensed company will not take. She sees the man from the licensed company do some kind of a test and shake his head. Won't take it. Then, when he has gone, Jess watches it being carted off to a shack at the farthest, most overgrown corner of Merkley's vast lot.

'Damned PCPs,' she hears one of Merkley's oafs swearing.

Then one day, just around closing, she watches Merkley's men load up the half-ton truck with four more drums of waste. She bikes home filled with fire.

It is the first time Walker has returned to the Teacup Falls since the night of no moon when he scared away the raccoon and discovered a house built out of dragonfly wings.

But this time Jess and he are armed with sleeping bags, hot milky coffee in a flask and egg sandwiches. They are armed with cameras and Steve's cellular phone. It is drizzling rain.

The truck comes at midnight. Walker phones the police and when he feels enough time has passed, when the cops must be on their way, he lets Jess loose. She slips from the safety of the Teacup and flits from tree to tree like some avenging fairy, flashing photographs as the sludge slops from the drum and Merkley's men yell curses into the night and try to hurry up, and spill goop on their pants and boots, and try to figure how many assailants they are up against for they feel utterly surrounded. Jess circles them everywhere, drawing a noose of popping camera flashes around their villainy. They are trapped by her.

The police arrive. The arrest is made.

'It'll be the car-squisher for those guys,' says Jess with evident satisfaction as she and Walker gather up their gear. Walker almost suggests they spend the night in this enchanted place. But they are

soaked. And through his elation poke the bones of a dreadful weariness.

He scans the ground with his flashlight to see if they've forgotten anything. His beam finds its way down to the dragonfly house. He stares at it, tattered a bit around the edges, dented by the rain, but still intact.

'What?' says Jess.

Then Walker stares at her with such obvious admiration that even in the dark she can feel it. She blushes and even in the dark he sees it.

'What holds it together?' he says.

Jess smiles. 'Just something I found in Mum's old actor's make-up kit,' she says. 'Spirit gum.'

The Rainbow Warrior

JAMES RIORDAN

Illustrated by Michael Foreman

WE HAVE lost many things: our lands, our forests, our game, our fish. We have lost our ancient faith, our ancient dress; some of the younger people have even lost their language and the legends and traditions of their ancestors. We cannot call those old things back to us; they will never come again. We may travel many days in the mountain trails and look in the secret places for them. They are not there. We may paddle many moons upon the sea, but our canoes will never enter the channel that leads to the yesterdays of our people. These things are lost.

Yet there is one thing that we have never lost, for we never had it. We were born without it. And among all the things we have learned from the white races this, at least, we have never acquired.

It is greed.

We look upon the greed of gain and wealth accumulated above the head of our poorer neighbours as one of the lowest sins to which a person may fall. It is thought disgraceful to have food if your neighbour has none. To be respected you must divide your possessions with the less fortunate.

A wise ancestor taught all Native Americans about the evil of greed and this is his story.

It all began with the coming of the White Man. He came with greedy, clutching fingers, greedy eyes, a greedy heart, to hunt for gold. The White Man fought, murdered, starved, went mad with love of that gold far up the Fraser River. *Tillicums* – our word for friends – were tillicums no more, brothers were foes, fathers and sons were sworn enemies. Their love of gold was a curse.

Many of our young men went as guides to the White Man to the farthest reaches of the Fraser. When they returned they brought back tales of greed and murder, and our old people shook their heads and said evil would come of it. But all our young men returned as they went – kind to the poor, kind to the hungry, sharing whatever they had with their tillicums. All except one.

This man, Shak-shak, 'the Hawk', by name, came back with hoards of gold nuggets, *chickimin* – money – everything. He was rich like the White Man and, like him, he kept it all to himself. He would count his chickimin, count his nuggets, gloat over them, toss them from hand to hand. He rested his head on them when he slept, he carried them about with him throughout the day. He loved them better than food, better than his tillicums, better than life itself.

The whole tribe grew angry. They said Shak-shak had caught the disease of greed. To cure him of it he must give a great *potlatch* – a grand feast – to share his riches with the poorer members of the tribe, divide them among the old and the sick.

But he jeered and laughed and told them, 'No, no, no!' and he went on loving and gloating over his gold.

It was then that the great spirit, Sagalie Tyee, spoke from out of the sky. 'Shak-shak, you have made yourself a loathsome creature. You will not listen to the cry of the hungry, to the call of the old and sick, you will not share your possessions; you have made yourself an outcast from your tribe and you have gone against the ancient laws of your people. Now I will make of you a creature hated by all.'

Shak-shak drew back in fear, his hands raised before his face as the Sagalie Tyee described his fate.

'You will have two heads, for your greed has two mouths. One bites the poor, and one gnaws at your own evil heart. And the fangs in those mouths are poison – poison that kills the hungry, and poison that kills your own manhood. Your evil heart will beat in the very centre of your foul body; he that pierces it will kill the disease of greed for ever.'

When the sun rose above the North Arm next morning, the people saw a giant sea serpent stretched across the surface of the waters. They were horror-struck. They hated the creature, they feared it, they loathed it. Day after day it lay there, its monstrous heads lifted out of the waters, its mile-long body blocking the entrance to the Narrows, all outlets from the North Arm. The chiefs called a council, the medicine men danced and chanted, but the monster, the Salt-chuck Oluk, never moved. It could not move, for it was the hated totem of what now rules the White Man's world – greed and love of chickimin.

But when the chiefs and medicine men had done all in their power and still the Salt-chuck Oluk lay across the waters, a handsome young boy approached them and reminded them of the words of the Sagalie Tyee:

'He who pierces the monster's heart will kill the disease of greed amongst his people for ever. Let me try to find this evil heart. Great men of my tribe, let me make war upon this creature. Let me rid my people of this plague.'

The boy was brave and handsome. His tribe called him the Tenas Tyee – the Little Chief – and they loved him dearly. All his wealth of fish and furs, of game and hykwa shells he gave to people who had none. He hunted for the old and sick; he tanned skins and furs for those whose feet were feeble, whose eyes were fading, whose blood ran thin with age.

'Let him go,' cried the people. 'This unclean monster can only be overcome by a pure heart; let him go.'

The chiefs and medicine men listened, then they made up their minds.

'Go,' they said, 'and fight this thing with your strongest weapons –

purity and kindness. We know that the customs of your ancestors are dear to you, the sayings and wisdom of the old people are the words you live by. Go and slay the monster.'

Tenas Tyee turned to his mother.

'I shall be gone for several days,' he said.

'While I'm away put fresh furs on my bed each day, even if I am not here to lie on them. If I know that my bed, my body and my heart are clean, I can overcome the serpent.'

'Your bed shall have fresh furs each morning,' said his mother.

Tenas Tyee went down to the waters, stripped off his clothes and, with only a buckskin belt to hold his hunting knife, he flung his lithe young body into the waves.

Days went by and he did not return. Now and then he could be seen swimming far out in mid-channel, searching for the serpent's evil, selfish heart. Finally, after many, many days, the people saw him rise out of the sea, climb to the summit of Brockton Point and greet the rising sun with outstretched arms.

Weeks went by. Months went by. And still Tenas Tyee swam each day, searching for the heart of greed. And each morning the sunrise gleamed on his slender copper-coloured body as he stood with outstretched arms at the summit of Brockton Point, greeting the coming day and then plunging from the clifftop into the sea.

Meanwhile, at his home on the North Shore, his mother dressed his bed with fresh furs each morning. The seasons drifted by: winter followed autumn, spring followed winter, summer followed spring. Yet it was four years before Tenas Tyee found the centre of the great Salt-chuck Oluk and plunged his hunting knife into its evil heart. In its death agony it writhed and thrashed through the Narrows, leaving a trail of black slime in the waters. Its huge body began to shrivel and wither away until nothing but the bones of its back remained; and they, sunbleached and